Youth
SOCCER
Drills

Third Edition

Jim Garland

HUMAN KINETICS

Library of Congress Cataloging-in-Publication Data

Garland, Jim, 1948-
Youth soccer drills / Jim Garland. -- Third edition.
     pages cm
1.   Soccer for children--Training.   I. Title.
GV944.2.G37 2014
796.334083--dc23
                            2013043566

ISBN-10: 1-4504-6823-3 (print)
ISBN-13: 978-1-4504-6823-7 (print)

Acquisitions Editor: Tom Heine; **Senior Managing Editor:** Anne Cole; **Associate Managing Editor:** Jan Feeney; **Copyeditor:** Patsy Fortney; **Graphic Designer:** Tara Welsch; **Cover Designer:** Keith Blomberg; **Photograph (cover):** © Human Kinetics; **Photographs (interior):** © Human Kinetics; **Photo Production Manager:** Jason Allen; **Art Manager:** Kelly Hendren; **Associate Art Manager:** Alan L. Wilborn; **Illustrations:** Susan Carson, Debra Garland; **Printer:** McNaughton & Gunn

Human Kinetics books are available at special discounts for bulk purchase. Special editions or book excerpts can also be created to specification. For details, contact the Special Sales Manager at Human Kinetics.

Printed in the United States of America   10 9 8 7 6 5 4 3 2 1

The paper in this book is certified under a sustainable forestry program.

Human Kinetics
Website: www.HumanKinetics.com

United States: Human Kinetics
P.O. Box 5076
Champaign, IL 61825-5076
800-747-4457
e-mail: humank@hkusa.com

Canada: Human Kinetics
475 Devonshire Road Unit 100
Windsor, ON N8Y 2L5
800-465-7301 (in Canada only)
e-mail: info@hkcanada.com

Europe: Human Kinetics
107 Bradford Road
Stanningley
Leeds LS28 6AT, United Kingdom
+44 (0) 113 255 5665
e-mail: hk@hkeurope.com

Australia: Human Kinetics
57A Price Avenue
Lower Mitcham, South Australia 5062
08 8372 0999
e-mail: info@hkaustralia.com

New Zealand: Human Kinetics
P.O. Box 80
Torrens Park, South Australia 5062
0800 222 062
e-mail: info@hknewzealand.com

E6131

I dedicate this book to Eloise Jane and all future little Garlands.

Contents

Drill Finder

Drill number	Title	Level of defense	Number of players	Time (min)	Page number
Spatial Concepts and Movement Drills					
1	Open Space Drill	None	1	5	4
2	Closed Space Drill	Subtle	2	5	6
3	Personal Space Drill	None	10 +	10	8
4	General Space Drill	None	10 +	10	10
5	Moving Vision Drill	None	10 +	10	12
6	Volcano Drill	None	4 +	5	14
7	Triangle Drill	None	1	30 sec	16
8	Copycat Drill	None	2	5	18
9	Monday Morning Traffic Drill	None	6+	5	20
10	Flag Tag Game	Subtle	2	5	22
11	Team Exchange Drill	None	12+	5	24
12	Jackrabbit Drill	None	3 +	10	26
13	Shirt Tag Game	Gamelike	3 +	10	28
14	Number Tag Game	Subtle	8 +	10	30
Dribbling Drills					
15	Fancy Footwork Drill	None	3 +	15	36
16	Follow-the-Leader Drill	None	10+	5	38
17	Freedom Drill	None	10 +	10	40
18	Freeze Drill	None	7 +	10	42
19	Is Anybody Home? Game	None	6 +	10	44
20	Triangle Tag Game	Subtle	7 +	10	46
21	Sprint Drill	None *	6 +	10	48
22	Partner Tag Game	Subtle	8 +	10	50
23	Intruders Game	Subtle	8 +	10	52
24	Circle Dribble Tag Game	Subtle	6	10	54
25	Shake-and-Take Drill	None *	1	10	56
26	Sprint Challenge Drill	Gamelike	3 +	10	58
27	Possession Drill	Gamelike	2	5	60

(continued)

Acknowledgments

Thanks to all of my fellow teachers, coaches, and clinicians, especially Jeffrey Tipping, and the staff at the National Soccer Coaches Association of America, who have been willing to share their ideas while helping to educate me in the game of soccer. A special thanks to Rob Bailey, who over the years has been a special friend and of great value in helping me develop new teaching strategies. Thanks to Gary Froman for his photography contributions in the earlier editions of this book and to Sharon Mitchell for her professional assistance with manuscript issues. I would also like to thank Linda Duncan for her editing efforts on this and other projects over the years. Thanks to my sons, Casey and Matthew, for their technological assistance. A special thanks to my wife, Debra, for her continued support and contributions of typing and artwork for this book.

Introduction

When I was a child, I loved playing. I was the kind of kid who hated rainy days and got angry when the sun went down in the evening. I still do. Rain or darkness meant playing would have to wait until another day. I was active, very active. I'm still active. Being still was for someone else. Being still meant being bored. None of that for me.

As I grew into adulthood and considered future employment, I knew I wanted two things: to stay active in sports and to help young people experience the same joys I had while at play. Being an elementary physical education teacher and coach was a natural fit for me. I was an elementary physical education teacher for 37 years, and I've coached from clinic-level teams through high school boys' varsity sports. In that time I've discovered two things about working with kids: they want to have fun, and if they don't understand what you're talking about, it's probably not their fault.

When working with children as a physical education teacher and coach, I've tried to remember how I felt as a child. I remember how much I hated listening to a coach talk for 20 minutes and then playing for only 10 minutes. Standing in long lines waiting for a turn during drills absolutely frazzled me.

These memories inspired me to write this book. I wanted to give youth soccer coaches a resource filled with activities that are easy to explain and fun for the kids, keeping even the most active kids satisfied. The drills I selected for this book meet these criteria. Besides providing drills to improve skill techniques, I have heavily emphasized movement concepts to improve the quality of players' movements. I have designed these drills for coaches of players ages 5 through 12. Players' parents and physical education instructors will also find this a handy reference. The book includes numerous demonstrations, drills, and games that will help players improve the quality of their play. Demonstrations are visual presentations, with or without accompanying dialogue by coaches or players, that show how to perform a skill or play a game. Drills are activities to improve play by repeating actions. Games differ from drills in two important ways: (1) games have rules and (2) games can be won. For the purpose of keeping things as straightforward as possible, the activities presented in this book are generally referred to as drills.

The book is divided into seven chapters. It begins with a chapter on space and movement that discusses open, closed, personal, and general space. These ideas are integrated with concepts of vision, direction, speed, and level into drills that promote the development of efficient movement. This chapter is exclusively for players in the 5- to 6-year-old range. Chapters 2 through 5 offer drills dealing with skill acquisition and tactical development. Drills are organized in progressions from least to most challenging. Those that are least challenging require less movement. Players often learn skills more quickly by practicing from a stationary position. As they become more successful, drills become more challenging. You can introduce movement; change the responsibility of players; or restrict time, space, or touches. You can add defensive pressure, beginning with subtle pressure and progressing to gamelike pressure. These chapters include drills that develop skills in dribbling, passing, collecting, heading, and shooting. The book does not include drills to develop the special skills of goalkeepers. Instead, it focuses on developing spatial, movement, and skill concepts for field players.

Chapters 1 through 6 include activities for individual, partner, small-group, and large-group drill work. Many drills contain more than one performance level. The higher the level, the more difficult the drill. Factors influencing the difficulty of the drill vary and may include adding players as defenders, changing spatial requirements, and combining movement with skills. Each drill is labeled according to its appropriateness: beginner (ages 5 and 6), advanced beginner (ages 7 and 8), intermediate (ages 9 and 10), and advanced (ages 11 and 12).

Many of the demonstrations, games, and drills use game markers, cones, and game spots to define boundaries. These items come in many sizes, shapes, and colors and may be purchased at almost any sporting goods store or online through various sporting goods companies. For the purpose of this book, large game markers are shown as the traditional cone shape, approximately 12 inches (30.5 cm) high. The small game markers are circular disc cones approximately 7 inches (17.8 cm) in diameter and 5 inches (12.7 cm) high. Game spots are flat, circular poly spot markers approximately 9 inches (22.9 cm) in diameter.

Chapter 6, Game Progressions, discusses a plan for implementing structured games according to players' readiness. The chapter identifies the concepts you can present at the 4v4, 5v5, 8v8, and 11v11 levels. Chapter 7, Using Drills in Practice, offers information about practice organization and includes practice plans for 5- to 6-year-olds, 7- to 8-year-olds, 9- to 10-year-olds, and 11- to 12-year-olds.

A drill finder is included to make the drills more accessible. It shows the level of defensive pressure, number of players, and time needed for each drill, as well as the page where it can be found. You can choose a skill or concept you are interested in, then easily select the drills that use the level of defensive pressure appropriate for your players. You can also use the information about the number of players and time required for each drill to plan and conduct efficient practices.

This book will help you help your players move more efficiently by using the drills that target direction, speed, and level. It is a resource to guide you in creating a logical order for teaching skills and concepts. The information about movement concepts will help you improve safety and reduce collisions during practices and games. In addition, you will develop a better understanding of what concepts you should present at each age level.

Many of the activities in this book are my original ideas, and some I collected by observing other coaches, clinicians, and teaching professionals. The book is not all-inclusive. Feel free to substitute some of your favorite drills where appropriate in the progression. Most important, have fun using this book. Your players will be grateful and will never have to say that the sun went down before they got their turn.

Note: If you use the metric system in your measurements, you can replace the number of yards with the same number of meters.

1

Spatial Concepts and Movement Drills

This chapter is designed to help beginning players (ages 5 and 6) move safely and efficiently. The development of spatial and movement concepts should be an integral part of beginning players' training. Often these concepts are neglected in favor of drills designed only for developing kicking, heading, and other ball skills. This is unfortunate. Practice sessions must be more balanced to incorporate drills that help players develop spatial and movement skills. A player who understands spatial and movement concepts moves with confidence and incurs fewer injuries as a result of collisions.

Spatial concepts are essential for tactical awareness, which helps a player decide where or when to move to support a teammate who has the ball. Understanding spatial concepts also allows a player in possession of the ball to make better tactical decisions concerning where and when to penetrate the defense using dribbling, passing, and shooting skills. Spatial concepts deal with where to move on the field. Training in spatial concepts includes teaching concepts of open space, closed space, personal space, general space, and vision:

- Open space—space that is unoccupied by players
- Closed space—space that is occupied by one or more players
- Personal space—the space that immediately surrounds a player
- General space—the entire area in which a player is allowed to function
- Vision—the entire field of vision a player must monitor, using scanning techniques to improve peripheral vision

Movement concepts deal with how players negotiate space. The development of movement concepts includes training in direction, speed, and level:

- Direction—the ability to maintain or change a pathway
- Speed—the ability to change the rate of motion
- Level—the position of a player's body in relation to the playing surface, such as in jumping (high level) or sliding (low level)

The drills presented in this chapter develop space and movement concepts progressively. They begin with demonstration drills of open and closed space. These are the fundamental concepts that guide much of the process of deciding where to move and where to play the ball next. These drills come first in the progression as a safety concern, to help reduce collisions.

Personal space and general space drills are second in the progression. These drills help players achieve field balance and avoid clustering on the field. Visual training follows, although it is also intertwined with demonstrations of open, closed, personal, and general space. The visual training drills develop good visual habits, such as breaking eye contact with the ground and scanning the periphery. These habits improve a player's range of vision on the field.

Next in the progression are elements of movement that help players create or deny space: direction, speed, and level. Players can create space (move to open space away from other players) or deny space (move toward other players to close space) by changing direction, speed, and levels more efficiently than their opponents do. All of the drills are presented developmentally, gradually increasing in difficulty based on how quickly players can execute the movements.

Many of the drills do not initially use a ball. In this way, beginning players gain confidence in their moving skills without having to control a ball. As your players demonstrate competence with movement, you can add a ball to increase the challenge.

OPEN SPACE DRILL

PURPOSE

To help players recognize how easy it is to move through unoccupied spaces. Use this drill to build a base of knowledge about the use of space, and refer to it in later teachings.

LEVEL

Beginner

EQUIPMENT

- 1 ball
- 2 large game markers

TIME

5 minutes

PROCEDURE

Level 1

1. Players huddle in a group.
2. Place two markers on a line about 10 yards apart.
3. One player stands by one of the markers.
4. The same player walks to the other marker (see figure).

Level 2

1. Players repeat steps 1 and 2 from level 1.
2. One player stands by one of the markers with a ball.
3. The same player dribbles the ball to the other marker.

Level 3

1. Players repeat steps 1 and 2 from level 1.
2. One player stands by one of the markers with a ball, and another player stands by the other marker.
3. The player with the ball passes the ball to the teammate who is standing by the other marker.

KEY POINTS

You have demonstrated how uncomplicated it is to move, dribble, and pass through open space. Young players will develop a more thorough understanding of space when you give them a visual demonstration. Refer to this drill often when explaining the effective use of space in training and game situations.

RELATED DRILL

Drill 2: Closed Space Drill

2   CLOSED SPACE DRILL

PURPOSE

To demonstrate how impossible it is to move, dribble, and pass through closed spaces.

LEVEL

Beginner

EQUIPMENT

- 1 ball
- 2 large game markers

TIME

5 minutes

PROCEDURE

Level 1

1. Players huddle in a group.
2. Place two markers on a line about 10 yards apart.
3. Player A stands by one of the markers.
4. Player B stands on the line at a point midway between the markers.
5. Player A walks on the line to the other marker.

Level 2

1. Players repeat steps 1 through 4 from level 1, except player A has a ball.
2. Player A dribbles the ball to the opposite marker without going off the line (see figure).

Level 3

1. Players repeat steps 1 through 4 from level 1, except player A has a ball.
2. Player C stands by the unoccupied marker.
3. Player A passes the ball to player C.

CLOSED SPACE DRILL

KEY POINTS

At level 1, player A will find this task impossible because player B, who has closed the space between the two markers, has blocked the pathway. At level 2, player A will not be able to dribble the ball through the space closed by player B. At level 3, player A will not be able to pass the ball through the space closed by player B.

Understanding open versus closed space should be a top priority for young players. Give them this visual demonstration of how impossible it is to move without the ball, to dribble with the ball, or to pass the ball through closed spaces. Refer to this drill when players begin clustering, colliding with teammates or opponents, or dribbling and passing into closed spaces. Explain to them the alternative—which is, of course, to use open space.

RELATED DRILL

Drill 1: Open Space Drill

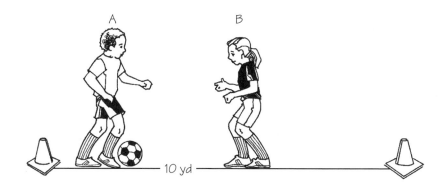

3   PERSONAL SPACE DRILL

PURPOSE

To develop an understanding that personal space is the space that immediately surrounds each player, and that player movement affects it.

LEVEL

Beginner

EQUIPMENT

9 large game markers

TIME

10 minutes

PROCEDURE

1. Divide players into groups of five. Players form four grids, each of which measures 5 yards by 5 yards, with one group in each grid. Number the grids 1 through 4.
2. Players move freely within each grid (see figure).
3. If a player touches another player, they both are frozen.
4. The players from grid 2 join the players from grid 1, and the players from grid 3 join the players from grid 4.
5. At this point, all frozen players become unfrozen and rejoin the other players.
6. Players move freely in their grids for about 30 seconds.
7. Finally, all of the players move to grid 1.
8. Players move freely for about 30 seconds (remind them not to touch anyone as they move).

KEY POINTS

As the players move in a grid with only four other players, maintaining their personal space should not be challenging. As the number of players in a space increases, movement becomes more difficult. When all the players are moving in a small space, it becomes al-

PERSONAL SPACE DRILL

most impossible to maintain their personal space or not to invade someone else's. During scrimmages and games, this drill can serve as a visual reminder that movement becomes difficult when players cluster. The result should be better spacing and less swarming as players learn to maintain their personal spaces.

RELATED DRILL

Drill 4: General Space Drill

4 GENERAL SPACE DRILL

PURPOSE

To develop an understanding that general space is the entire area in which a player can function and that, within this general space, larger spaces are easier to negotiate than smaller ones.

LEVEL

Beginner

EQUIPMENT

4 large game markers

TIME

10 minutes

PROCEDURE

1. All players scatter within a grid identified by four game markers approximately 20 yards apart (see figure).
2. Players move freely through the entire grid.
3. Expand the size of the grid to 50 yards by 50 yards.
4. Players move freely through the larger grid.
5. After the players move in both grids, discuss with them in which grid they found it easier to move.

KEY POINTS

The personal space drill showed how increasing the number of players in a space affected a player's personal space and movement. This drill demonstrates how increasing the size of the space makes player movement easier, because there is more time to make decisions about changing direction, speed, and levels. Players should recognize that by using all the spaces within the general space properly, they maintain field balance and move more freely.

RELATED DRILLS

Drill 1: Open Space Drill
Drill 2: Closed Space Drill
Drill 3: Personal Space Drill

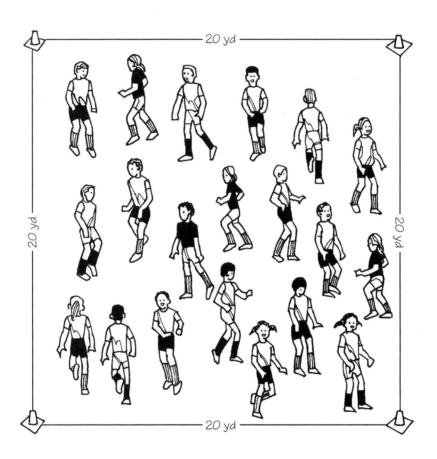

5   MOVING VISION DRILL

PURPOSE

To develop good visual habits when negotiating space with and without the ball.

LEVEL

Beginner

EQUIPMENT

- 1 soccer ball for each player
- 4 large game markers

TIME

10 minutes

PROCEDURE

Level 1

1. Players scatter within a 30- by 30-yard grid (see figure).
2. On your signal, players move freely throughout the grid by walking to a four-count rhythm.
3. Players take one step with the left foot, one step with the right, one step with the left again, looking left as they step, and one step with the right, looking right as they step.
4. Players verbalize the movement by chanting, "Left, right, look left, look right."
5. Players repeat the drill, this time while jogging.

Level 2

Players repeat level 1 steps while using a ball.

KEY POINTS

Movement affects a player's vision. You must train players to look constantly in the direction in which they are moving and to scan to the right and left so they can negotiate space efficiently. Practice this visual drill before adding a ball. Adding a ball adversely affects vision. Beginning players, especially, like to look down at the ball to keep it under control. Insist that they look left and right during the sequence so they break eye contact with the ball. If they seem out of control, ask them to slow down.

RELATED DRILLS

None

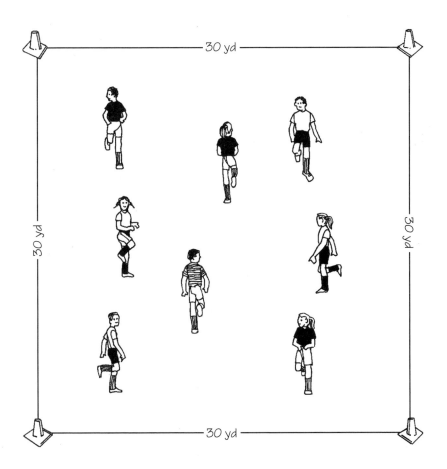

VOLCANO DRILL

PURPOSE

To develop an understanding of changing direction.

LEVEL

Beginner

EQUIPMENT

4 large game markers plus 1 small game marker for each player

TIME

5 minutes

PROCEDURE

1. Players scatter throughout a 20- by 20-yard grid.
2. Within the grid, scatter approximately 16 markers, or one for each player. Players will pretend these markers are volcanoes (see figure).
3. On your signal, players move through the grid.
4. As players approach a volcano, they must quickly change direction to avoid being burned by any lava.
5. Challenge the players to see how many volcanoes they can pass in 30 seconds.

KEY POINTS

This drill helps players understand feinting. Demonstrate that, to change direction quickly, players should flex one leg slightly and quickly push off the inside of the same foot. Encourage them to exaggerate this push-off in a lateral direction. Players can apply more force in this lateral direction by flexing the leg. Incorporate various body parts (including the head, shoulders, and arms) in this shifting of weight from one direction to another. Have players experiment with combinations of feints—for example, feint right, left, and then quickly back to the right.

VOLCANO DRILL

RELATED DRILL

Drill 7: Triangle Drill

7 TRIANGLE DRILL

PURPOSE

To assess how well players are able to change direction and speed.

LEVEL

Beginner

EQUIPMENT

3 large game markers

TIME

30 seconds

PROCEDURE

1. Place three game markers 10 feet (3 m) apart in a triangle formation (see figure).
2. On your signal, players move laterally to touch one marker, pivot, move laterally to the next marker, pivot again, and then move laterally to the third marker.
3. Players repeat this action for 30 seconds.
4. Players count the number of markers touched.

KEY POINTS

Use this simple drill to assess players' performance of lateral movements and of changes in direction and speed. Adding the pivot enables them to develop the change-of-direction skills often required in game situations. You should not compare players' results. The purpose of this drill is not to determine which player performs the best, but simply to show players their individual improvement.

RELATED DRILLS

Drill 8: Copycat Drill
Drill 9: Monday Morning Traffic Drill
Drill 10: Flag Tag Game

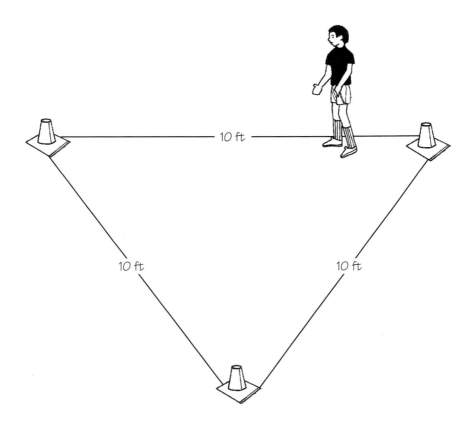

10 ft

10 ft

10 ft

8   COPYCAT DRILL

PURPOSE

To demonstrate how changing speed and direction creates space.

LEVEL

Beginner

EQUIPMENT

4 large game markers

TIME

5 minutes

PROCEDURE

1. Two players stand side by side on a line of a 20- by 20-yard grid (see figure).
2. On your signal, player A begins to move forward, changing speed as she goes.
3. Player B looks at player A and copies her movements.
4. If player A comes to a stop, she can reverse directions and go back toward the line where she started, again changing speed.
5. Player A may choose to change speed and direction several times.
6. When you signal to stop, player B should still be beside player A.
7. Have players reverse roles several times during the drill.

KEY POINTS

Encourage your players to use short bursts of speed and changes of direction to create space between themselves and their opponents.

RELATED DRILL

Drill 9: Monday Morning Traffic Drill

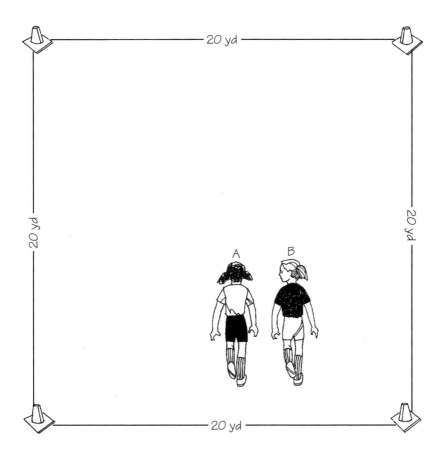

9 MONDAY MORNING TRAFFIC DRILL

PURPOSE
To demonstrate how changing speed and direction creates space.

LEVEL
Beginner

EQUIPMENT
4 large game markers

TIME
5 minutes

PROCEDURE
1. Scatter players with partners in a 15- by 15-yard grid.
2. Player B is the driver of the car. Player A is the backseat passenger whom player B is driving to work (see figure).
3. Player B moves through the grid, changing speed and direction and avoiding other drivers who are also on their way to work.
4. The backseat passengers are responsible for following their drivers closely, always maintaining an arm's-length distance from them.
5. Have players reverse roles several times during the drill.

KEY POINTS
This drill can be equivalent to typical Monday morning traffic during rush hour, including traffic jams and fender benders. Encourage all players to change speed and direction—and monitor the movements of other pairs—to avoid collisions.

RELATED DRILLS
Drill 8: Copycat Drill
Drill 10: Flag Tag Game

10   FLAG TAG GAME

PURPOSE

To demonstrate how changing speed and direction creates space.

LEVEL

Beginner

EQUIPMENT

- 4 large game markers for every 2 players
- 1 flag belt for each player

TIME

5 minutes

PROCEDURE

Level 1

1. Position two players at opposite sides of a 10- by 10-yard grid (see figure).
2. Players wear flag belts.
3. On your signal, player A approaches player B and tries to pull her flag.
4. Player B tries to change speed and direction to get to the opposite side of the grid without having her flag pulled.
5. Player A earns 1 point if she can grab player B's flag.
6. If player B can get to the opposite side of the grid without having her flag pulled, she earns 1 point.
7. The player who earns 5 points first is the winner.
8. Players then reverse roles.

Level 2

1. Place six players, two teams of three each, in a 20- by 20-yard grid.
2. On your signal, players try to steal the opposite team's flags.
3. A player whose flag is pulled must partner up with a teammate before again helping to grab flags.
4. The team that captures all of the other team's flags first is the winner.

KEY POINTS

Encourage player A to close the space toward player B by making a bending run at her and by assuming a good defensive stance. A bending run means that the defender approaches the opponent using a curved pathway instead of a straight line. A curved pathway allows the defender to guide the opponent toward a part of the square that reduces the amount of territory to defend (e.g., toward a teammate or a boundary line). Spacing of players is important at level 2.

RELATED DRILLS

Drill 8: Copycat Drill
Drill 9: Monday Morning Traffic Drill

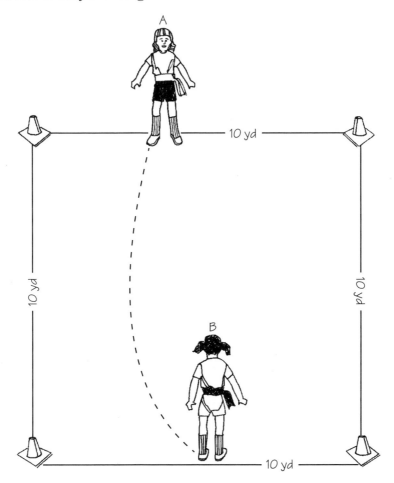

11   TEAM EXCHANGE DRILL

PURPOSE

To demonstrate how to change speed and direction to avoid closed spaces.

LEVEL

Beginner

EQUIPMENT

4 large game markers

TIME

5 minutes

PROCEDURE

1. Divide players into four equal groups. Position one group on each side of a 10- by 10-yard grid (see figure).
2. On your signal, players exchange places with the group opposite them.
3. Players vary their movements by walking, jogging, and running.

KEY POINTS

All players will be moving to get to the opposite side of the grid. Moving at a different speed from that of the adjacent group will be essential to avoid closed spaces. This drill is more gamelike because it simulates the challenge of movement during games. Many times, teammates and opponents will be clustered while moving in opposite directions toward each other. Other times, teammates and opponents will cross paths with each other. Avoiding collisions by changing speed and direction will reduce the possibility of injury.

RELATED DRILL

Drill 13: Shirt Tag Game

10 yd

10 yd

10 yd

10 yd

12   JACKRABBIT DRILL

PURPOSE

To develop balance while changing levels.

LEVEL

Beginner

EQUIPMENT

4 large game markers, plus 1 small game marker per player

TIME

10 minutes

PROCEDURE

1. Scatter game markers in a 20- by 20-yard grid.
2. On your signal, players move freely through the grid (see figure).
3. As they approach a marker, players jump with two feet as high as they can over the marker, landing lightly on both feet. As they land, they quickly change direction.
4. After repeating this action several times, players jump, taking off with one foot and landing on both feet.
5. Players jump again, this time taking off with two feet and landing on the left foot; they then push off and change direction to the right.
6. Players repeat this action and then switch, landing on the right foot and changing direction to the left.

KEY POINTS

Encourage players to use their arms to generate momentum when they jump and to balance themselves when they land.

RELATED DRILLS

None

13   SHIRT TAG GAME

PURPOSE

To develop an understanding of direction, speed, and level and their relationships to movement.

LEVEL

Beginner

EQUIPMENT

- 1 scrimmage shirt for each player
- 4 large game markers
- Several balls

TIME

10 minutes

PROCEDURE

Level 1

1. Players scatter in a 20- by 20-yard grid.
2. Each player has a scrimmage shirt tucked into the back of her pants (see figure).
3. On your signal, players travel through the grid, trying to grab the tucked scrimmage shirt of another player.
4. Players try to grab as many scrimmage shirts as possible in a two-minute period.
5. If a player's scrimmage shirt is pulled, she must go outside the grid and do 10 touches on a ball before returning to the game. At the end of two minutes, stop and give all players a chance to get ready for a new game.

Level 2

1. Players repeat level 1, steps 1 and 2.
2. Each player moves through the grid with a ball while trying to collect scrimmage shirts.

KEY POINTS

Encourage players to avoid closed spaces as they change direction, speed, and levels. Change the specific skill that eliminated players must execute for each game—for example, 10 rollovers or 8 step-overs. For variety, divide the group into two teams and have them play Team Shirt Tag. When playing shirt tag at level 2, players who lose control of the ball while trying to collect a scrimmage shirt must go outside the grid.

RELATED DRILL

Drill 14: Number Tag Game

14   NUMBER TAG GAME

PURPOSE

To develop an understanding of direction, speed, and level and their relationships to movement.

LEVEL

Beginner

EQUIPMENT

- 4 large game markers
- 1 ball for each player (level 2)

TIME

10 minutes

PROCEDURE

Level 1

1. All players line up on one side of a 30- by 30-yard grid.
2. Each player has a number from 1 to 4.
3. Two players (defenders) stand between the line of players and the opposite line, which is safe territory (see figure).
4. Defenders each call a random number simultaneously.
5. The player whose number is called tries to travel through open space to the safe line.
6. A player who is tagged must sit down.
7. When the next number is called, that player can try to free the players sitting down by touching them while on the way to safe territory.
8. A player who is freed must try to get to the safe zone without being tagged.

Level 2

1. Players repeat level 1, except each player on the line must reach the safety zone while dribbling a ball.
2. A player whose ball is touched by a defender must sit down.

NUMBER TAG GAME **14**

KEY POINTS

Encourage your players to be in control as they change direction, speed, and levels. Defenders should make bending runs as they try to capture players, and should avoid having two defenders chase one player (unless he is the only one left). During level 2 action, encourage numbered players to shield the ball from defenders while traveling toward the safety zone.

RELATED DRILL

Drill 13: Shirt Tag Game

31

2

Dribbling Drills

Players who master spatial and movement skills are able to travel through space efficiently. Using these skills when in possession of the ball, however, requires devoting time to improving ball skills. Players can work on these skills in formal practice sessions and in informal sessions at home. The drills in this chapter will help them develop one of these ball skills—dribbling. Dribbling means applying controlled touches to the ball, using various surfaces of the foot, so that the ball remains within playing distance of the dribbler. It is one of the ways to advance the ball through open space or to create open spaces when a player is tightly defended. Players can dribble in a straight line, using the inside or outside of the foot, when moving through open space.

Negotiating closed spaces requires changing the position of the ball in relation to the body as well as changing the position of the body in relation to the ball (feinting). The following are examples of changing the position of the ball in relation to the body:

- Push-away—using a surface of the foot to quickly move the ball away from the body and stop it
- Pull-back—using a surface of the foot, usually the sole, to bring the ball back toward the body and stop it
- Rollover—using a surface of the foot on the ball to roll the ball forward, backward, or sideways

The following dribbling moves are examples of changing the position of the body in relation to the ball:

- Step-over—stepping over the ball to its left with the right foot and pivoting back to the right on the right foot (also done with the left foot going to the right of the ball and pivoting back to the left)
- Scissors—stepping over the ball, feinting left, and touching ball to the right with the outside of the right foot (also done with an opposite feinting action)
- Walkover—simply walking over the ball and turning

The dribbling drills in this chapter progress from least to most difficult. They include the following:

- Stationary dribbling drills
- Dribbling and movement with no defensive pressure
- Dribbling with subtle defensive pressure
- Dribbling with gamelike defensive pressure

Performing a skill from a stationary position is simpler than performing it while moving. When a player is stationary, her visual focus is not affected by negotiating space with other players. Therefore, she can devote all of her visual attention to the skill, not to how and where to move. After players gain some confidence with dribbling from a stationary position, challenge them by placing them in motion—without the added burden of defensive pressure. This will give them the time and space needed to develop these skills. As they become more competent with dribbling, add defensive pressure. As the degree of difficulty increases, players cannot focus only on the technical aspects of dribbling (the *how to*), but must also concentrate on tactical elements (the *when* and *where*). Increase the pressure gradually from subtle to gamelike pressure. Give players opportunities to practice penetrating dribbling skills, because the role of the first attacker (the player with the ball) is to penetrate the defense. Small-sided drills provide such opportunities during practice sessions.

When using these drills, exercise patience as players progress from a slow, methodical pace to a more gamelike pace. Expecting players to perform new moves under pressure before they are ready will lead to frustration and failure and may cause them to abandon any effort to master new moves. Let them improve at their own rates.

Improved dribbling skills will enable players to keep the ball longer, penetrate the defense, create spaces for passing and shooting, and relieve defensive pressure.

15   FANCY FOOTWORK DRILL

PURPOSE

To improve the ability to control the ball while in a stationary position, with no defensive pressure.

LEVEL

Beginner, advanced beginner

EQUIPMENT

- 1 soccer ball for each player
- 4 large game markers

TIME

15 minutes

PROCEDURE

1. Players (with balls) scatter in a 20- by 20-yard grid (see figure).
2. While stationary, players practice controlled touches on the ball.
3. Players can combine these touches in various ways to change speed, direction, or levels. Encourage players to change the position of the ball in relation to their bodies with push-aways, pull-backs, rollovers, and so forth.
4. Players then practice changing body position in relation to the ball with step-overs, scissors, walkovers, and so forth.

KEY POINTS

There should be time for hundreds of touches on the ball during each practice. Encourage players to explore ways to move the ball using the inside, outside, sole, and heel of each foot. Players may mirror moves that you demonstrate, but encourage them to create new combinations of moves as well. As they touch the ball, encourage them to maintain good vision constantly. For variety, and to reduce fatigue, have them work with partners. Have one partner work on skills for a minute and then give the ball to the other partner, who does the same. Change formations using triangles, circles, and so forth, to add variety to this drill. Give players time to develop these skills from a stationary position, without movement into other spaces and without defensive pressure. Players should also practice these moves at home as part of a daily routine.

RELATED DRILLS

Drill 17: Freedom Drill
Drill 18: Freeze Drill
Drill 19: Is Anybody Home? Game

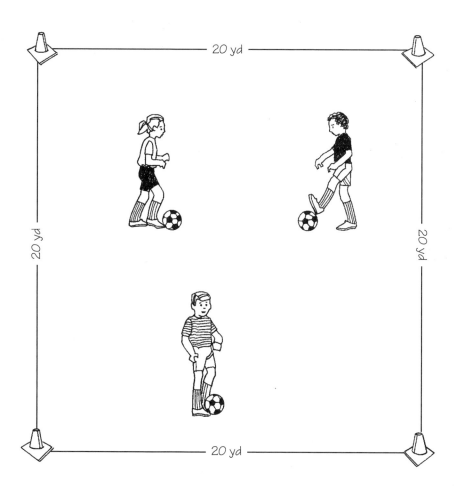

16 FOLLOW-THE-LEADER DRILL

PURPOSE

To develop dribbling skills while negotiating space with no defensive pressure.

LEVEL

Beginner, advanced beginner, intermediate

EQUIPMENT

- 1 soccer ball for each player
- 4 large game markers

TIME

5 minutes

PROCEDURE

1. Players divide into lines of four or five players, in a 20- by 20-yard grid (see figure).
2. The first player in line is the leader and begins moving through the grid. The rest of the players follow while dribbling their balls.
3. On your signal, the last person in line pushes his ball out approximately 5 yards in front of the leader, sprints after it, and becomes the new leader.
4. The new last person repeats this action on your next signal.

KEY POINTS

Encourage ball control by discussing the force exerted on the ball when various parts of the foot are used to touch it. Review the proper use of the general space provided so that lines of players don't move into the same space. As players achieve greater control over their movements, have them perform this drill without your signals.

RELATED DRILL

Drill 21: Sprint Drill

FOLLOW-THE-LEADER DRILL 16

17   FREEDOM DRILL

PURPOSE

To develop dribbling skills while negotiating space with no defensive pressure.

LEVEL

Advanced beginner

EQUIPMENT

- 1 soccer ball for every 2 players
- 5 large game markers

TIME

10 minutes

PROCEDURE

1. Partners space themselves around a circle approximately 30 yards in diameter (see figure).
2. On your whistle, the partner with the ball travels into the circle, practicing her own moves as she encounters other players who are doing likewise.
3. After a minute of moving, the player with the ball returns and gives the ball to her partner, who repeats the action.
4. Players have complete freedom to use any of their own moves during this drill.

KEY POINTS

Encourage players to use a variety of moves to change direction, speed, and levels as they negotiate space. Refer to the demonstration on spatial and movement concepts included in drills 1 to 4 in chapter 1 if players are moving into closed spaces. This drill is the next step in the dribbling progression, because it requires players to use their own moves to travel through the space provided. This gives them the freedom to develop skills without defensive pressure.

RELATED DRILLS

Drill 15: Fancy Footwork Drill
Drill 18: Freeze Drill
Drill 19: Is Anybody Home? Game

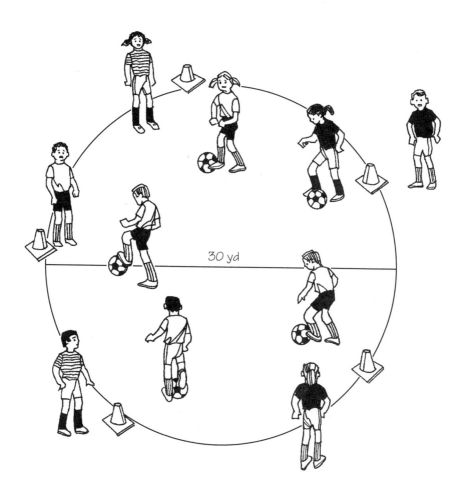

30 yd

18   FREEZE DRILL

PURPOSE

To develop dribbling skills while negotiating space with no defensive pressure.

LEVEL

Advanced beginner

EQUIPMENT

- 1 soccer ball for each player
- 4 large game markers

TIME

10 minutes

PROCEDURE

1. Players scatter in a 20- by 20-yard grid.
2. All players move freely through the grid, each with a ball (see figure).
3. When you signal by blowing a whistle, the players must freeze by bringing their balls to a complete stop.
4. Variations of this drill might include touching the ball with any body part on one side of the body, freezing while touching the ball with more than one body part, or freezing at various levels.

KEY POINTS

This drill gives players the opportunity to develop their own moves while negotiating space without defensive pressure. Encourage them to use body parts on their nondominant side. Freezing at various levels might include straight-legged, crouching, or kneeling positions.

RELATED DRILLS

Drill 15: Fancy Footwork Drill
Drill 17: Freedom Drill
Drill 19: Is Anybody Home? Game

19   IS ANYBODY HOME? GAME

PURPOSE
To develop dribbling skills with no defensive pressure.

LEVEL
Beginner

EQUIPMENT
- 1 soccer ball for each player
- 3 red, 3 blue, and 3 yellow game spots
- 4 large game markers

TIME
10 minutes

PROCEDURE
1. Scatter players with balls in a 30- by 30-yard grid as shown in the figure.
2. Space three red, three blue, and three yellow game spots in the grid.
3. On your signal, players dribble their ball throughout the grid, weaving their way among the game spots and the other players.
4. When you blow the whistle, the players stop.
5. Ask, "Is anyone home in the blue house?"
6. Players scramble to touch the blue game spots. The first player to touch one of the three blue spots is safe. All others must run around one of the corner grid markers and return to their balls.
7. Blow your whistle again to restart the dribbling action.
8. Again, blow the whistle to stop the action. This time, call out a different color (e.g., "Is anyone home in the red house?").
9. Repeat the action for each of the three colors.

IS ANYBODY HOME? GAME 19

KEY POINTS

Encourage players to use controlled touches on the ball and various surfaces of their feet. Remind them to always use good vision when involved in a group activity of this nature by touching their balls then looking up to avoid collisions with other players.

RELATED DRILLS

Drill 15: Fancy Footwork Drill
Drill 17: Freedom Drill
Drill 18: Freeze Drill

20   TRIANGLE TAG GAME

PURPOSE

To develop dribbling skills with subtle defensive pressure.

LEVEL

Beginner

EQUIPMENT

- 1 soccer ball for each player
- 1 red jersey
- 4 large game markers
- 15 small game markers

TIME

10 minutes

PROCEDURE

1. Position players with balls in a 30- by 30-yard grid as shown in the figure. Also included in the grid are five 2- by 2-yard triangles made with small game markers.

2. Position player A in the grid holding a red scrimmage jersey and without a ball.

3. On your signal, player A runs anywhere within the grid trying to tag players. Players tagged by player A must freeze. Players who lose control of the ball so that it goes out of the grid must retrieve the ball, get back in the grid, and freeze.

4. A frozen player must stay frozen unless until another player can dribble the ball between the frozen player's legs. This action unfreezes the frozen player.

5. The triangles are free spaces for the players with balls. Player A is not allowed inside them. Only one player is allowed in a triangle at a time.

6. If a triangle is occupied, player A may go up to the triangle and count, "One thousand one, one thousand two," until she counts to one thousand ten. The player in the triangle must leave by the time player A counts to one thousand ten.

7. Play continues until all players are frozen or a preset time limit has expired.

8. Choose another player to be player A (the tagger) and have players repeat the game.

KEY POINTS

Encourage players to use good visual scanning techniques to know where the tagger is at all times. Challenge them to find open spaces within the grid in which to dribble. If the game becomes too difficult for the tagger, reduce the number of triangles or add a second tagger.

RELATED DRILLS

Drill 23: Intruders Game
Drill 29: Dribble Chase Game
Drill 32: Invasion Game
Drill 33: Four-Grid Scramble Game

21   SPRINT DRILL

PURPOSE

To develop dribbling skills and speed for negotiating space with no defensive pressure.

LEVEL

Intermediate, advanced

EQUIPMENT

- 1 soccer ball for each player
- 4 large game markers

TIME

10 minutes

PROCEDURE

1. Players scatter in a 20- by 20-yard grid, each with a ball.
2. The players travel through the grid until they hear your whistle.
3. On that signal, players dribble their balls as fast as they can out of the grid (see figure).
4. They continue dribbling as fast as they can until they hear a second whistle.
5. On the second whistle, the players dribble as fast as they can back to the grid, where they continue to travel through the grid at a moderate pace.

KEY POINTS

Present this drill only when players have developed sufficient ball control skills. Encourage them to push the ball away to open spaces at a distance of 5 to 7 yards, then sprint to the ball. Kicking the ball as far as they can and sprinting after it is not the purpose of this drill. After players become more skilled with speed dribbling, add players in the grid without balls. On your signal, the players without balls chase the players who are speed dribbling.

RELATED DRILL

Drill 16: Follow-the-Leader Drill

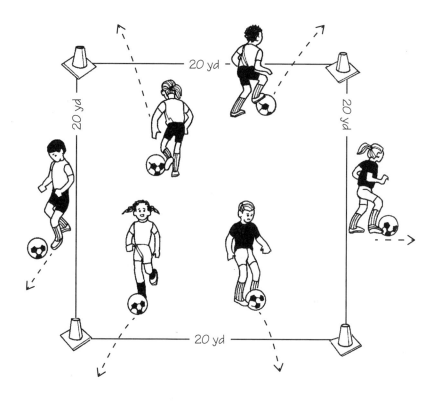

PARTNER TAG GAME

PURPOSE

To develop dribbling skills while negotiating space with no defensive pressure.

LEVEL

Beginner or advanced beginner

EQUIPMENT

- 1 soccer ball for every 2 players
- 4 large game markers

TIME

10 minutes

PROCEDURE

1. Position sets of partners, each with a ball, in a 20- by 20-yard grid as shown in the figure.
2. One set of partners does not have a ball. They are "it."
3. The set of partners without a ball chase the partners with balls trying to tag them.
4. If either of the two partners are tagged, they must freeze.
5. The frozen partners stay frozen until another set of partners can unfreeze them by dribbling their ball between the legs of one of the frozen players.
6. The game ends when all players are frozen or a preset time limit expires.
7. Choose another partner set to be "it," and have players repeat the game.

KEY POINTS

Encourage partners to use soft touches when dribbling to control the ball. Challenge them to use good visual techniques to scan the grid to find the taggers and reduce collisions with other partner groups.

RELATED DRILLS

Drill 24: Circle Dribble Tag Game
Drill 31: Two-Team Dribble Tag Game

INTRUDERS GAME

PURPOSE

To develop dribbling skills with subtle defensive pressure.

LEVEL

Beginner

EQUIPMENT

- 5 soccer balls
- 4 large game markers
- 6 small game markers

TIME

10 minutes

PROCEDURE

1. Position players in a 30- by 30-yard grid as shown in the figure.

2. On your signal, the players without balls turn their backs to the players with balls.

3. Give a hand signal to the players with balls to begin dribbling toward the players with their backs turned.

4. The players with balls try to dribble through one of the 2-yard-wide chutes spaced between game markers 3 and 4 without being tagged. If they are successful, they earn 1 point and return to a space between game markers 1 and 2 to repeat the action.

5. If you blow the whistle during the action, all players with balls must return to spaces between game markers 1 and 2, by dribbling, while being chased by the players without balls. Dribbling players who are tagged put their balls on the sideline and become taggers.

6. Players assume starting positions with all taggers positioned between game markers 3 and 4 and all dribblers between game markers 1 and 2.

7. The game ends when no dribblers remain.

8. The dribbler who scores the most points is the winner.

9. Select new taggers and begin the game again.

KEY POINTS

This is a fun way for beginning players to practice dribbling skills. If players are being tagged too easily, reduce the number of taggers, increase the size of the grid, or blow the whistle before the dribblers get too close to the taggers.

RELATED DRILLS

Drill 20: Triangle Tag Game
Drill 29: Dribble Chase Game
Drill 32: Invasion Game
Drill 33: Four-Grid Scramble Game

24 CIRCLE DRIBBLE TAG GAME

PURPOSE

To develop dribbling skills with subtle defensive pressure.

LEVEL

Advanced beginner or intermediate

EQUIPMENT

- 2 soccer balls
- 4 large game markers for every 6 players

TIME

10 minutes

PROCEDURE

Level 1

1. Place six players in a 10- by 10-yard grid.
2. Four players form a circle.
3. Two players, each with a ball, stand outside the circle on opposite sides (see figure).
4. Designate one of these players as the tagger.
5. On your signal, the tagger has 30 seconds to tag the other player with a ball, while both players are dribbling.
6. The tagger may cut through the circle, but the player being chased may not.

Level 2

1. Players repeat level 1, steps 1 through 6.
2. While the tagger is chasing the other player, players who have formed the circle move as a unit to shield the player being chased from the tagger.

KEY POINTS

Players need to use good visual techniques to know when the tagger has changed direction. Changing direction and speed frequently will help the player being chased.

RELATED DRILLS

Drill 22: Partner Tag Game
Drill 31: Two-Team Dribble Tag Game

25   SHAKE-AND-TAKE DRILL

PURPOSE

To develop the dribbling skills used to create space and go to the goal (under defensive pressure in levels 2 and 3).

LEVEL

Advanced beginner, intermediate, advanced

EQUIPMENT

- 1 soccer ball for each player
- 1 large game marker for each goal
- 4 goals

TIME

10 minutes

PROCEDURE

Level 1

1. Place a marker 40 yards from the goal.
2. A player dribbles toward the marker, executes an individual move to create space (a scissors move, for example), and then goes to the goal and shoots (see figure).

Level 2

1. Place two markers 40 yards from the goal, about 5 yards apart.
2. A defender stands on a line between the markers and tries to tackle the ball away from the attacker as the attacker attempts to go between the markers to the goal.

Level 3

1. Player A stands 40 yards from the goal.
2. A defender stands 30 yards from the goal.
3. The ball is passed to player A.
4. When player A touches the ball, the defender may pursue him.
5. Player A uses his own moves to create space to go to the goal.

KEY POINTS

Allow players to develop their own moves with imaginary pressure (the marker in level 1) until they succeed. When their skills have improved to the point of needing more of a challenge, add a defender who can move only laterally (level 2). This change adds subtle pressure. A defender applies gamelike pressure at level 3. Do not rush players through their progressions. Use as many goals as are available, or make temporary goals, so players have many opportunities to score.

RELATED DRILLS

None

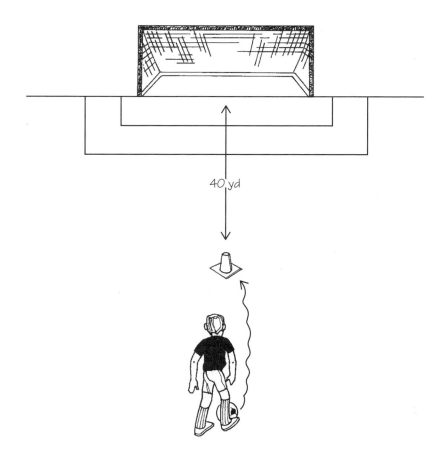

26 SPRINT CHALLENGE DRILL

PURPOSE

To develop dribbling skills and speed when confronted with game-like defensive pressure.

LEVEL

Intermediate, advanced

EQUIPMENT

- 1 soccer ball for every 3 players
- 4 goals

TIME

10 minutes

PROCEDURE

Level 1

1. Player A stands about 5 yards behind player B.
2. Pass the ball forward.
3. Player B must collect the ball, sprint toward the goal, and shoot before the defender, player A, can catch her.
4. Variations include serving balls at different speeds, from various directions, and at different levels.

Level 2

1. Players repeat level 1, steps 1 through 4.
2. Add a goalkeeper to increase the defensive pressure (see figure).

KEY POINTS

Encourage players to push the ball out 5 to 7 yards to maintain both speed and control. In level 2, restrict the goalkeeper by not allowing her to come off the goal line. As players' skills increase, add more goalkeeping pressure.

RELATED DRILLS

Drill 27: Possession Drill
Drill 28: Partner Dribble Game
Drill 30: Change-of-Direction Game

Coach   B

A

27 POSSESSION DRILL

PURPOSE

To develop shielding and dribbling techniques under gamelike pressure.

LEVEL

Beginner, intermediate, advanced

EQUIPMENT

- 1 soccer ball
- 4 large game markers

TIME

5 minutes

PROCEDURE

1. Position four game markers to make a 10- by 10-yard grid.
2. Position two players inside the grid, one with the ball and the other as a defender (see figure).
3. On your signal, the player with the ball combines shielding and dribbling techniques to keep possession of the ball for 30 seconds. If the player with the ball loses possession before 30 seconds elapse, the drill is over.
4. After 30 seconds or loss of possession, players reverse roles.

KEY POINTS

A key element to success for any team involved in a game such as soccer is to keep possession of the ball. A team retains possession partly because individual team members know how to shield and dribble to create spaces for penetrating the defense. Penetration is the role of the first attacker (i.e., the player with the ball). During this drill, encourage offensive players to keep their bodies between the ball and the defender. When they are shielding, insist that they try to position themselves "sideways on" to the defender. This position creates the greatest distance between the defender and the ball.

RELATED DRILLS

Drill 26: Sprint Challenge Drill
Drill 28: Partner Dribble Game
Drill 30: Change-of-Direction Game

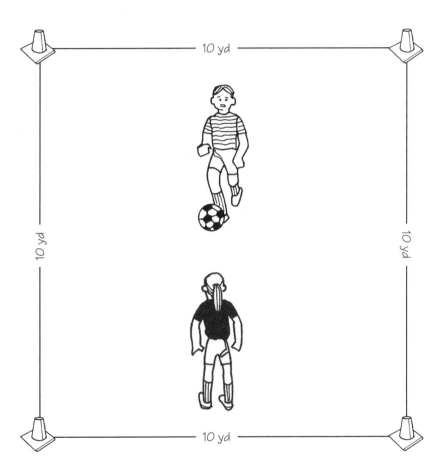

28   PARTNER DRIBBLE GAME

PURPOSE

To develop dribbling skills to create space under gamelike defensive pressure.

LEVEL

Advanced beginner, intermediate, advanced

EQUIPMENT

1 soccer ball and 4 large game markers for every 2 players

TIME

10 minutes

PROCEDURE

1. In a 10- by 10-yard grid, one partner stands on a line with a ball and the other partner stands on the opposite side of the square (see figure).
2. Player A passes the ball to player B.
3. When player B receives the ball, player A pursues her in an effort to close her space and touch the ball or to force her out of the grid.
4. If player A touches the ball, she earns 1 point.
5. If player B dribbles safely to the opposite line, she earns 2 points.
6. The first player to earn 6 points is the winner.
7. Players reverse roles.

KEY POINTS

The offensive player in this drill earns more points for being successful because this is an offensive drill. Encourage the offensive player to use a variety of moves to create space.

RELATED DRILLS

Drill 26: Sprint Challenge Drill
Drill 27: Possession Drill
Drill 30: Change-of-Direction Game

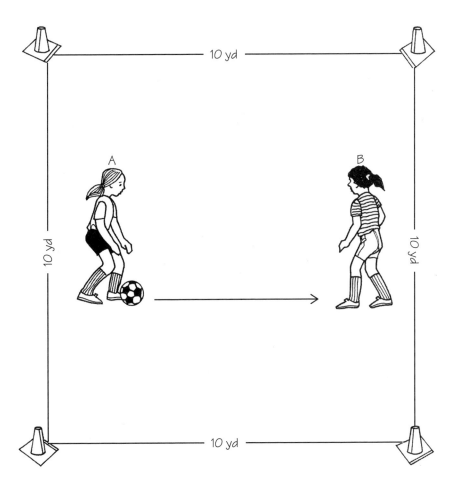

29   DRIBBLE CHASE GAME

PURPOSE

To develop dribbling skills and speed with subtle defensive pressure.

LEVEL

Advanced beginner, intermediate

EQUIPMENT

- 2 soccer balls
- 4 large game markers

TIME

10 minutes

PROCEDURE

1. Position two players, each with a ball, on diagonal corners of a 10- by 10-yard grid as shown in the figure.
2. On your signal, the players dribble around the grid in an attempt to tag each other.
3. When you signal again, players must reverse direction.

KEY POINTS

This drill challenges players to maintain possession of the ball while dribbling. Encourage them to apply controlled touches to the ball. Emphasize not sacrificing control of the ball for speed of execution. During practice sessions you can set up several grids and have multiple games of Dribble Chase being played simultaneously. This is also an excellent activity for players to engage in when arriving to practice. Instead of waiting for everyone on the team, the first two players who arrive can begin, the second two players can then begin, and so on.

DRIBBLE CHASE GAME

29

RELATED DRILLS

Drill 20: Triangle Tag Game

Drill 23: Intruders Game

Drill 32: Invasion Game

Drill 33: Four-Grid Scramble Game

30   CHANGE-OF-DIRECTION GAME

PURPOSE

To develop dribbling skills and speed when confronted with game-like defensive pressure.

LEVEL

Advanced beginner, intermediate

EQUIPMENT

- 6 soccer balls
- 4 large game markers

TIME

15 minutes

PROCEDURE

1. Position two lines of three players on one side of a 10- by 20-yard grid as shown in the figure.
2. The last players in each line enter the grid (to reduce competition to be first in line).
3. The coach serves a ball to the two players in the grid.
4. The player gaining possession of the ball tries to dribble it over either end line designated by game markers 1 and 2 or the end line designated by game markers 3 and 4, while being defended by the player who did not gain possession.
5. When you blow the whistle, the player in possession of the ball must change direction and try to dribble the ball over the end line in the opposite direction.
6. If the defender steals the ball, she may try to dribble over either end line.
7. Each time a player dribbles over the end line, she earns 1 point for her team. After a point is scored, the next set of players enter the grid. The coach will serve a ball to continue play. The first team to earn 10 points is declared the winner.

CHANGE-OF-DIRECTION GAME **30**

KEY POINTS

You can make this game a lot of fun by blowing the whistle and having players change direction frequently. Serve a variety of passes for players to control including rolling, bouncing, and airborne passes. The grid for this game is intentionally narrow to help players defend the dribbler more efficiently. If offensive players are struggling, increase the width of the grid.

RELATED DRILLS

Drill 26: Sprint Challenge Drill
Drill 27: Possession Drill
Drill 28: Partner Dribble Game

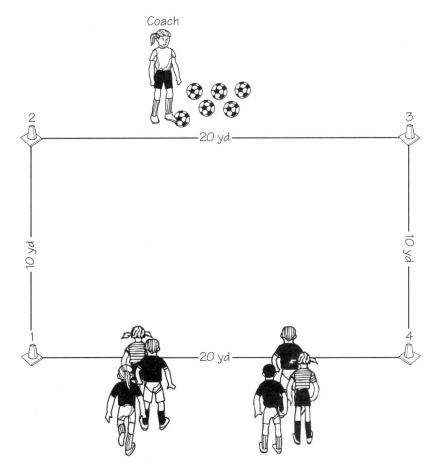

31 TWO-TEAM DRIBBLE TAG GAME

PURPOSE

To develop dribbling skills and speed with subtle defensive pressure.

LEVEL

Intermediate, advanced

EQUIPMENT

- 1 soccer ball
- 3 red and 3 blue scrimmage jerseys
- 12 large game markers

TIME

10 minutes

PROCEDURE

1. Position three players from each team as shown in the figure.
2. On your signal, player D dribbles the ball toward player A. At the same time, player E assumes the position vacated by player D next to game marker 4.
3. Player D continues to dribble the ball until she touches it to player A. Player A then dribbles and touches the ball to player E.
4. Player B takes the position vacated by player A next to game marker 1. When appropriate, player C takes the position vacated by player B, and player F takes the position vacated by player E.
5. After player D touches the ball to player A as described in step 3, she continues to run around game marker 2 and chase player A to try to tag her. If player D tags player A, she earns 1 point for her team.
6. If player A is not tagged, she continues dribbling and touches the ball to player E. Player A continues her run around game marker 5 and chases player E to attempt to tag her.

7. When a player is tagged, the game begins again with the tagged player's team starting the dribble from either game marker 1 or 4.

8. Have players play a game to 5 points, or see which team can score the most points in five minutes.

KEY POINTS

This is an excellent game to help develop dribbling speed in open space. Encourage players to push the ball away to open spaces at a distance of 5 to 7 yards and sprint after it. If players are being tagged too easily, increase the distance between game markers 1 and 2 and between game markers 4 and 5.

RELATED DRILLS

Drill 22: Partner Tag Game
Drill 24: Circle Dribble Tag Game

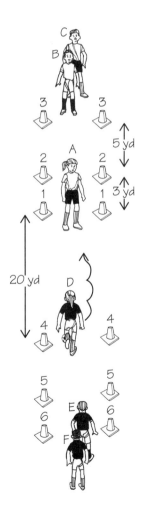

INVASION GAME

PURPOSE

To develop dribbling skills with subtle defensive pressure.

LEVEL

Beginner

EQUIPMENT

- 4 soccer balls
- 4 large game markers
- 1 red jersey

TIME

10 minutes

PROCEDURE

1. Position players in a 30- by 30-yard grid as shown in the figure. Player A wears the red jersey.

2. On your signal, player A, the invader, tries to tag any of the players in the groups who have possession of the ball (i.e., player B).

3. Player B may dribble anywhere in the grid and use his two partners as shields.

4. The other two players in each group, who are holding hands, may move and try to position themselves between player A and their team member with the ball. They must continue to hold hands during this shielding action.

5. If player A tags a player in possession of a ball, all players in the group must freeze with their legs spread.

6. The frozen group must stay frozen until a dribbler from any unfrozen group dribbles a ball through the legs of each of the frozen players at which time they become unfrozen and return to action.

7. The game continues until all groups are frozen.

8. Players then change roles (dribblers, shielders, and invader) and repeat the action.

KEY POINTS

Beginning players will have lots of fun with this game. Encourage players to use soft touches to control the ball and use good visual techniques to move to spaces where their partners can shield them from the tagger.

RELATED DRILLS

Drill 20: Triangle Tag Game
Drill 23: Intruders Game
Drill 29: Dribble Chase Game
Drill 33: Four-Grid Scramble Game

33   FOUR-GRID SCRAMBLE GAME

PURPOSE

To develop dribbling techniques and tactics while negotiating space under subtle defensive pressure.

LEVEL

Intermediate, advanced

EQUIPMENT

- 12 soccer balls
- 16 large game markers

TIME

10 minutes

PROCEDURE

1. Position game markers to make four 20- by 20-yard grids.
2. Place four players in each grid, three with a ball, one without (see figure).
3. On your signal, the player without the ball chases the other players in an attempt to touch a ball.
4. If the player without a ball touches another player's ball or causes a player to dribble the ball out of the grid, the ball becomes the possession of the player without the ball.
5. The new player without a ball must then chase another player to gain possession of a ball, but may not regain possession from the player who caused him to lose possession.

KEY POINTS

This drill offers hundreds of touches and maximum activity while developing the technical aspect of the first attacker's dribbling skills. Using four grids with four players (instead of one large grid with 16 players) enables them to concentrate on dribbling skills, without the visual distraction of numerous players. Using a defender to provide subtle defensive pressure adds tactical decision making to the task. To challenge more highly skilled players, reduce the size of the grid (so players can develop dribbling skills in tight spaces) or add a second defender (player without a ball). If you add a second defender, increase the number of players in the grid to five.

RELATED DRILLS

Drill 20: Triangle Tag Game
Drill 23: Intruders Game
Drill 29: Dribble Chase Game
Drill 32: Invasion Game

SIX-GOAL GAME

PURPOSE

To develop dribbling techniques and tactics under gamelike defensive pressure.

LEVEL

Intermediate, advanced

EQUIPMENT

- 3 soccer balls
- 12 large game markers
- 6 red and 6 blue jerseys

TIME

10 minutes

PROCEDURE

1. Position three pairs of game markers in a line, 20 yards apart, to make three 2-yard-wide goals.

2. On the opposite side of the field, 40 yards from the first line of markers, position three other sets in a line, 20 yards apart, to make three other 2-yard-wide goals (see figure).

3. In the middle of the field, position three red and three blue players.

4. Position one blue player 5 yards behind each blue goal and one red player 5 yards behind each red goal. These players are not goalies. They are servers who restart the action after each score.

5. On your signal, players from each team try to dribble through any of their opponents' goals, scoring 1 point for each successful attempt. The ball must be dribbled and not passed through the goal.

6. After scoring, the offensive player becomes a defender, and the defender becomes the new offensive player. The server behind the goal puts the ball in play, passing it to the new offensive player.

7. Play continues for 5 minutes, at which time the players in the middle switch roles with the servers.

8. The team with the most points after 10 minutes is the winner.

KEY POINTS

The role of the first attacker (player with the ball) is to penetrate the defense. This game gives players opportunities to develop the technical aspects of dribbling through lots of touches on the ball, as well as opportunities for tactical (decision-making) development. By allowing players to dribble through any of the opponents' three goals instead of just one, this game encourages lots of changes of direction with the ball. To add some variety, have the servers restart play with throw-ins.

RELATED DRILLS

None

3

Passing and Collecting Drills

One of the most difficult tasks coaches have is developing their players' ability to connect consecutive passes. To acquire this ability, players must develop efficient passing and collecting techniques (the *how*) and tactical knowledge (the *when* and *where*). Collecting is the ability to gather in and control the ball using various parts of the body. Technical passing skills may be introduced early in the process of player development, and should be more heavily emphasized in the later stages of development. Tactical knowledge generally increases with experience. Give players opportunities through small-sided drills to learn to pass through open spaces instead of spaces closed by defenders. They can also learn when it is appropriate to pass the ball to a teammate's feet and when they should play the ball through space to connect with a teammate making a run. Knowing which teammate to pass to is also important. Players should make passing choices in this order:

1. Pass to a teammate who is in position to score.
2. Pass to penetrate the defense and advance the ball in a forward direction.
3. Pass to a teammate who can relieve defensive pressure so the team can retain possession of the ball.

Passing choices may be limited by a player's physical ability, skill level, and field position, or even by the quality of the opponent. Passing choices increase when players move off the ball, improve their skills, take risks, and maintain good field vision.

This chapter presents drills in a progression: (1) stationary passes to a stationary target; (2) stationary passes to a moving target; (3) moving passes to a stationary target; (4) moving passes to a moving target; (5) passing skills with subtle pressure; and (6) passing skills with gamelike pressure.

The drills emphasize the development of long- and short-passing techniques. Encourage players to develop short-passing techniques that will allow them to deliver accurate, crisp, flat passes. Instruct them to rotate the heel of the kicking foot toward the target in a locked position, allowing the large inside surface of the foot to contact the ball. The foot should contact the upper half of the ball, which provides topspin on the ball and makes it stay low (flat) to the ground. Encourage players to exaggerate their follow-through with a high knee lift of the kicking leg. For longer kicks, players should position the nonkicking foot a little farther back and away from the ball. This provides full leg extensions as the foot strikes the bottom of the ball. The ankle of the kicking foot should be turned slightly downward during these longer kicks. The kicking foot should stay low during the follow-through. In the first stage of this progression, players learn how hard or softly they must kick a ball for it to travel a certain distance. Players will learn to judge leg speed and to kick the ball with varying degrees of force based on the situation.

The first stage of the passing progression requires a stationary player to pass to a stationary target. Drills at this level develop proper passing techniques by excluding performance inhibitors such as motion and defensive pressure.

When players have improved their passing techniques, challenge them by adding motion. Begin by having them pass to a moving target. This requires that they understand the relationships among the speed of the target player, the distance of the target, and the speed and angle of the pass. This scenario becomes more challenging in the next phase of the progression, as you put passers in motion. Now they must compute all the factors involved in passing to a moving target, while negotiating space themselves. Beginning players may find this a visual nightmare. To limit frustration, have them proceed slowly at first and gradually increase their speed.

The final stage of the progression adds defensive pressure, which reduces the time and space in which to make decisions. Progress from subtle to gamelike defensive pressure according to your players' ability.

As players become more competent with passing skills, the quality of their play should improve. They should begin using soccer terminology that refers to the direction of the pass:

- Through pass—splits two defenders
- Square pass—played to another player laterally (to the side)
- Back pass—played in a backward direction, often referred to as a drop

With good communication and improved passing skills, your players' style of play will change from an individualistic, do-it-yourself style in which they always want to dribble, to one that is more team oriented and intentional.

79

35   PARTNER PASSING DRILL

PURPOSE

To develop passing accuracy and collection skills from a stationary passer to a stationary target with no defensive pressure.

LEVEL

Beginner, advanced beginner

EQUIPMENT

- 1 soccer ball for every 2 players
- 4 large game markers

TIME

10 minutes

PROCEDURE

Level 1

1. Players scatter within a 30- by 30-yard grid.
2. Partners should be about 10 yards apart.
3. Players pass to their partners, who collect the balls and return the passes (see figure).
4. Encourage players to speak aloud the sequence of "collect, look, look right, and pass."
5. Players repeat the sequence, this time looking left, or looking left and right, before returning the pass.

Level 2

1. Players repeat level 1, steps 1 through 5.
2. Vary this activity by using three players in a triangle or several players in a circle formation.
3. After a stationary player passes to a stationary target, she runs to that player's space.

KEY POINTS

Beginning players should stop the ball before returning it to their partners. Encourage them to relax the part of the body used for stopping the ball, which will have a cushioning effect. Stopping the ball improves the accuracy of passes, because it's easier to strike a stationary ball than one in motion. Level 2 incorporates movement after the pass. This helps to establish the concept that the passer should continue to be a player (instead of becoming a spectator) after passing. Later, this movement will lead to executing wall passes.

RELATED DRILLS

Drill 50: Partner Thruway Drill
Drill 37: Thread-the-Needle Drill
Drill 43: Spaceman Drill
Drill 46: Two-Cone Drill
Drill 53: Pass-Dribble-Pass Drill
Drill 54: First-Touch Drill

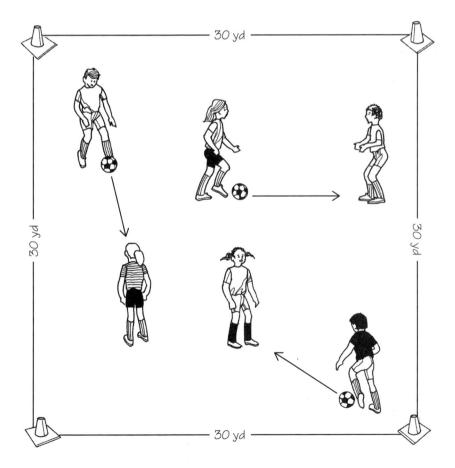

36   KNOCKOUT GAME

PURPOSE

To develop passing accuracy with no defensive pressure.

LEVEL

Beginner

EQUIPMENT

- 1 soccer ball for each player
- 6 large game markers
- 1 colored soccer ball

TIME

10 minutes

PROCEDURE

1. Position two teams of four players around a circle as shown in the figure.
2. On your signal, players kick their balls at the colored soccer ball in the center of the circle.
3. Whichever team hits the colored ball enough times to make it cross the line on the other team's half of the circle is the winner.

KEY POINTS

Designate one player from each team to go into the circle and pass balls back out to teammates waiting outside the circle. You may choose to have them play several two-minute games. In this version, when two minutes are up, a team wins if the colored ball is on the other team's side and not completely out of the circle.

RELATED DRILLS

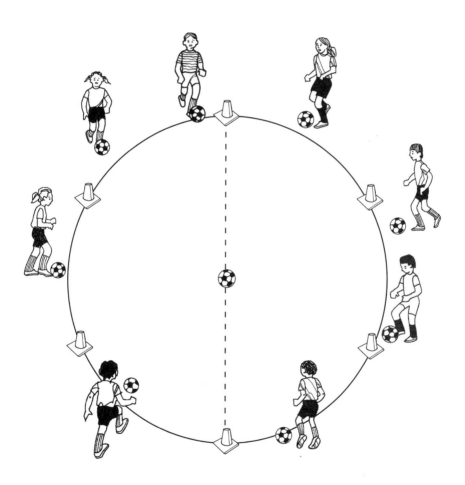

37 THREAD-THE-NEEDLE DRILL

PURPOSE

To improve passing accuracy and collection skills from a stationary passer to a stationary target with no defensive pressure.

LEVEL

Beginner, advanced beginner

EQUIPMENT

1 soccer ball and 2 large game markers for every 2 players

TIME

5 minutes

PROCEDURE

1. Partners with two cones between them scatter over the field (see figure).
2. Place cones initially about 3 or 4 yards apart.
3. Partners pass the ball to each other between the markers.
4. Have some fun with this drill by making it a game.
5. On your signal, players begin passing.
6. After each successful pass, they take one step backward.
7. If the ball does not go between the markers, players must return to the starting point and begin again.
8. After two minutes, stop and ask partners to notice how far apart they are.

KEY POINTS

Begin this drill with partners approximately 10 yards apart. As players' skill level improves, increase the distance between the players and decrease the distance between the markers. To assess player performance, count how many times partners are able to pass the ball between the markers in 20 attempts. Make sure that players collect the ball and bring it to a stop before returning the pass.

RELATED DRILLS

Drill 35: Partner Passing Drill
Drill 50: Partner Thruway Drill
Drill 43: Spaceman Drill
Drill 46: Two-Cone Drill
Drill 53: Pass-Dribble-Pass Drill
Drill 54: First-Touch Drill

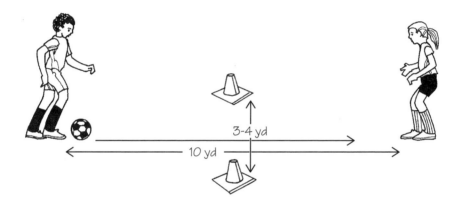

38   THE ROUND-UP GAME

PURPOSE

To develop dribbling and passing skills with no defensive pressure.

LEVEL

Advanced beginner

EQUIPMENT

- 10 soccer balls
- 6 large game markers
- 16 small game markers

TIME

10 minutes

PROCEDURE

1. Position players in a 40- by 40-yard grid as shown in the figure.
2. Position 10 soccer balls on the center line.
3. On your signal, players run to the centerline, dribble a ball back into the 10- by 10-yard grid on their side, and then kick the ball to the other team's side.
4. Players continue by rounding up (collecting) any ball found on their side, dribbling it to the closest grid on their side, and kicking it to the other team's side.
5. After two minutes, stop the game and count the number of soccer balls on each side.
6. The team with fewer soccer balls on its side is declared the winner.
7. Replace the soccer balls on the centerline and have players repeat the game.

KEY POINTS

Encourage players to collect the balls on their side as fast as they can. Challenge them to look carefully to find spaces that are not occupied by players on the other team when kicking balls to the other team's side. You can vary this drill by limiting players to using only their left feet or their right feet.

RELATED DRILLS

Drill 36: Knockout Game
Drill 51: Three-Player Passing Drill
Drill 49: Return-to-Sender Drill
Drill 40: Two-Team Passing Challenge Game
Drill 55: Three-Team Passing Drill

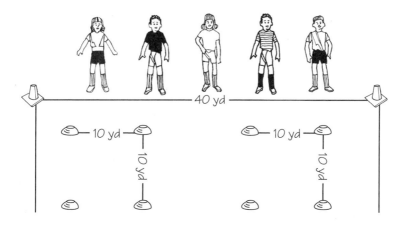

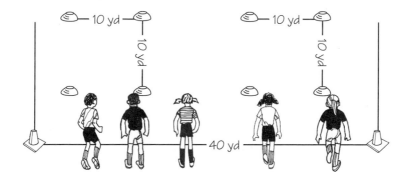

39   GOOD-BYE DRILL

PURPOSE

To develop passing accuracy and collection skills from a stationary passer to a stationary target, and to initiate movement after the pass with no defensive pressure.

LEVEL

Beginner

EQUIPMENT

1 soccer ball and 4 large game markers for every 3 players

TIME

5 minutes

PROCEDURE

Level 1

1. Position three players in three corners of a 10- by 10-yard grid (see figure).
2. Player A passes to player B, says "Good-bye," and travels to the unoccupied corner of the grid.
3. Player B then passes to player C, says "Good-bye," and travels to the corner vacated by player A.
4. Players repeat this action several times.

Level 2

1. After players feel comfortable with the spacing provided by the 10-yard grid, remove the game markers.
2. Instruct the players to now travel in general space among other groups of three, repeating the movements from level 1.

KEY POINTS

Encourage players to deliver crisp, flat passes that are easy to collect. Players should pass and move quickly to the open space. Reinforce this action (i.e., pass and move) in scrimmages and games. At level 2, encourage players to move through open spaces as they negotiate other players and to maintain 10-yard spacing.

RELATED DRILLS

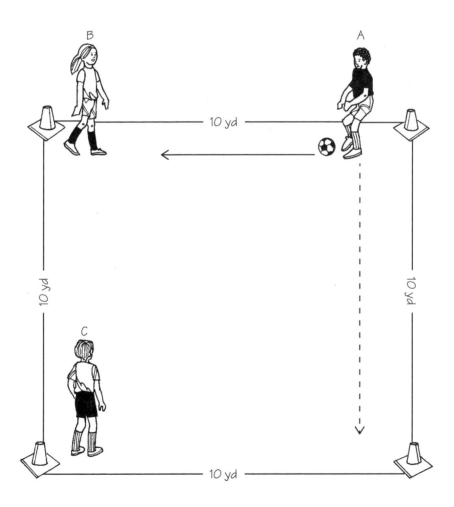

40 TWO-TEAM PASSING CHALLENGE GAME

PURPOSE

To develop passing accuracy and collection skills using long passes with no defensive pressure.

LEVEL

Intermediate, advanced

EQUIPMENT

- 2 soccer balls
- 4 red and 4 blue scrimmage jerseys
- 16 large game markers

TIME

15 minutes

PROCEDURE

1. Position one player from each team in a 10- by 10-yard grid as shown in the figure.

2. The red player in grid 1 and the blue player in grid 3 have balls and begin the action.

3. On your signal, the ball is passed from grid 1, to grid 2, to grid 3, to grid 4, and so on.

4. If a player does not pass the ball inside the next grid, he must retrieve the ball as quickly as possible and repeat his attempt to pass it into the next grid. If he misses the second attempt, the teammate he is attempting to pass to retrieves the ball and continues play.

5. The first team to pass the ball to all four grids twice is the winner.

KEY POINTS

Encourage players to follow through with the kicking foot staying low to the ground while striking the bottom of the ball. Emphasize full leg extensions to maximize power for kicking these longer distances. As a variation, have teams see how many grids they can pass to in a three-minute time frame, or have them play until one team "laps" the other.

RELATED DRILLS

Drill 36: Knockout Game
Drill 38: The Round-Up Game
Drill 51: Three-Player Passing Drill
Drill 49: Return-to-Sender Drill
Drill 55: Three-Team Passing Drill

41 CIRCLE COLLECTION DRILL

PURPOSE

To develop passing accuracy and collection skills from a stationary passer to a moving target with no defensive pressure.

LEVEL

Advanced beginner, intermediate

EQUIPMENT

6 soccer balls for every 9 players

TIME

10 minutes

PROCEDURE

1. Six players form a circle.
2. Each player has a ball (see figure).
3. Three other players are in constant motion inside the circle.
4. When an inside player makes eye contact with a player on the circle, that player passes the ball to the inside player.
5. The inside player returns the pass to the player who passed it and moves to another space to collect another pass.
6. Players forming the circle exchange places with the inside players every one to two minutes.

KEY POINTS

Caution players moving inside the circle to pass through open spaces. Players on the inside should collect, look, and make good decisions concerning their next pass. This will help to avoid striking another moving player with the ball.

RELATED DRILLS

Drill 39: Good-Bye Drill
Drill 42: Hello Drill
Drill 44: Pendulum Drill
Drill 47: Line Drill
Drill 48: Two-Touch Drill
Drill 52: Four-Corner Passing Drill
Drill 45: Turning Drill

42 HELLO DRILL

PURPOSE

To develop passing accuracy and collection skills from a stationary passer to a moving target with no defensive pressure.

LEVEL

Beginner

EQUIPMENT

1 soccer ball and 4 large game markers for every 3 players

TIME

5 minutes

PROCEDURE

Level 1

1. Each of three players stands in a corner of a 10- by 10-yard grid (see figure).
2. Player C, closest to the unoccupied corner and not in possession of the ball, moves to the unoccupied corner and says "Hello."
3. Player A, the one with the ball, passes to player C.
4. Player B moves to the space vacated by player C and then receives a pass from player C.

Level 2

1. As players become comfortable with spacing, remove the game markers.
2. Several groups of players can move in one large grid, repeating level 1 action.

KEY POINTS

Encourage players moving to a new space to give an oral reminder to the passers. In this drill they should be saying "Hello." For the sake of consistency, you may want your players to say "Space." The moving players should wait until the passer has controlled the ball and has made eye contact before initiating any movement. Discuss with players how delivering a soft pass to a player who is coming toward the ball aids the collection process.

RELATED DRILLS

Drill 39: Good-Bye Drill
Drill 41: Circle Collection Drill
Drill 44: Pendulum Drill
Drill 47: Line Drill
Drill 48: Two-Touch Drill
Drill 52: Four-Corner Passing Drill
Drill 45: Turning Drill

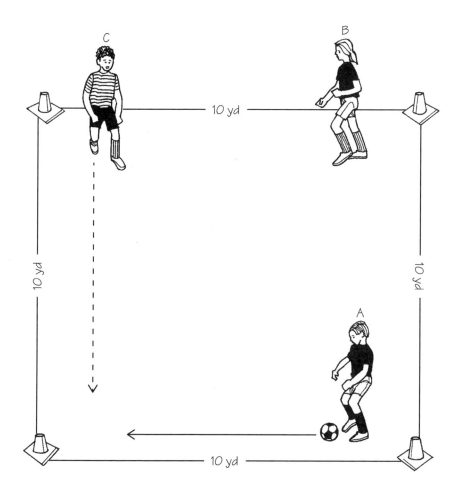

SPACEMAN DRILL

PURPOSE

To develop passing accuracy and collection skills from a stationary passer to a moving target with no defensive pressure.

LEVEL

Advanced beginner, intermediate

EQUIPMENT

1 soccer ball and 3 large game markers for every 2 players

TIME

5 minutes

PROCEDURE

Level 1

1. Position two players in a triangle identified by markers placed 10 yards apart.
2. Each player occupies a corner of the triangle (see figure).
3. The player without the ball runs to the unoccupied corner of the triangle and says loudly, "Space!"
4. The player with the ball passes it to the moving player.
5. The player who passed the ball moves to the unoccupied corner to receive a return pass.
6. Players repeat this action several times.

Level 2

1. Remove game markers.
2. Have partners travel through general space among other partners while using a triangular pattern with 10-yard spacing.

KEY POINTS

Encourage players moving to open space to make eye contact with the passer to ensure that the passer has the ball under control to make a pass. Instruct the passer to lead the player moving to space by passing the ball slightly ahead of him so that he doesn't have to break stride to collect the ball. Timing runs and communicating well are important to the success of this drill.

RELATED DRILLS

Drill 35: Partner Passing Drill
Drill 50: Partner Thruway Drill
Drill 37: Thread-the-Needle Drill
Drill 46: Two-Cone Drill
Drill 53: Pass-Dribble-Pass Drill
Drill 54: First-Touch Drill

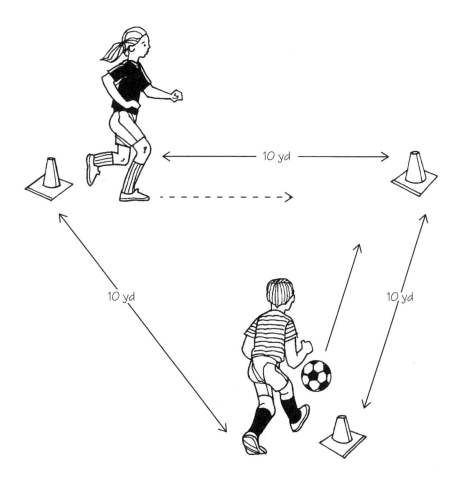

44   PENDULUM DRILL

PURPOSE

To develop passing accuracy and collection skills from a stationary passer to a moving target with no defensive pressure.

LEVEL

Advanced beginner, intermediate

EQUIPMENT

2 soccer balls and 4 large game markers for every 3 players

TIME

10 minutes

PROCEDURE

1. Position three players in a 10- by 10-yard grid (see figure).
2. Two players, standing on one side of the grid, each have a ball.
3. A third player is on the opposite side.
4. The player without the ball moves to the unoccupied corner.
5. As she moves, the player on that side passes the ball.
6. The moving player collects the ball and returns it to the player who passed it to her, and then runs to the corner she just left to receive a pass from the other player.
7. Players continue this back-and-forth movement.
8. After one minute, players switch roles.
9. After their skills improve, players can play the pendulum game by counting how many passes they can make in one minute.

KEY POINTS

Encourage players to make flat passes with the correct amount of force so the ball is easy to collect. Discuss how the speed of the receiving player affects how far the passer must lead the pass.

PENDULUM DRILL

44

RELATED DRILLS

Drill 39: Good-Bye Drill
Drill 41: Circle Collection Drill
Drill 42: Hello Drill
Drill 47: Line Drill
Drill 48: Two-Touch Drill
Drill 52: Four-Corner Passing Drill
Drill 45: Turning Drill

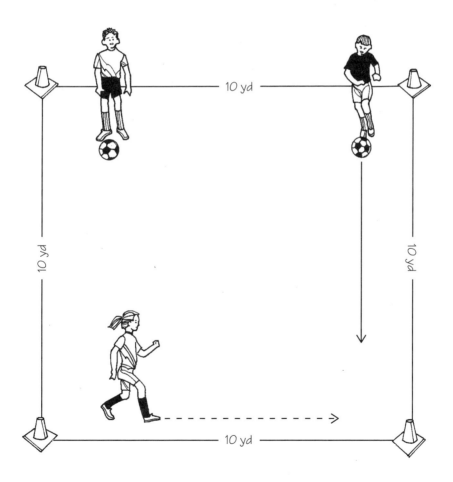

45 TURNING DRILL

PURPOSE

To develop passing accuracy and collection skills from a stationary passer to a moving target with no defensive pressure.

LEVEL

Intermediate, advanced

EQUIPMENT

- 1 soccer ball
- 8 large game markers

TIME

10 minutes

PROCEDURE

1. Position three players behind each set of game markers (labeled 1 and 2), which are spaced 20 yards apart (see figure).
2. On your signal, player A makes a diagonal run and assumes a sideways position (back to the sideline).
3. Player B passes to player A, who collects the ball with the foot that is closer to her marker (game marker 1) when in the sideways position. In this example it would be the right foot.
4. Player A then passes the ball to player C.
5. Player A moves to the end of the line behind game marker 2.
6. After player C collects the pass from player A, player B makes a diagonal run and assumes a sideways position. Player B's diagonal run is to the opposite side of the grid from player A's run.
7. Player C passes the ball to player B.
8. Player B collects the ball with the foot that is closer to his marker.
9. Player B then passes the ball to player D.
10. Player B moves to the end of the line next to game marker 1.

KEY POINTS

Players should practice collecting passes in a way that increases the speed of play. Players who can collect passes in a sideways position when there is no defensive pressure can turn and change direction more efficiently. Collecting while in the sideways position also increases a player's vision, enabling him to make the next decision with the ball faster.

RELATED DRILLS

Drill 39: Good-Bye Drill
Drill 41: Circle Collection Drill
Drill 42: Hello Drill
Drill 44: Pendulum Drill
Drill 47: Line Drill
Drill 48: Two-Touch Drill
Drill 52: Four-Corner Passing Drill

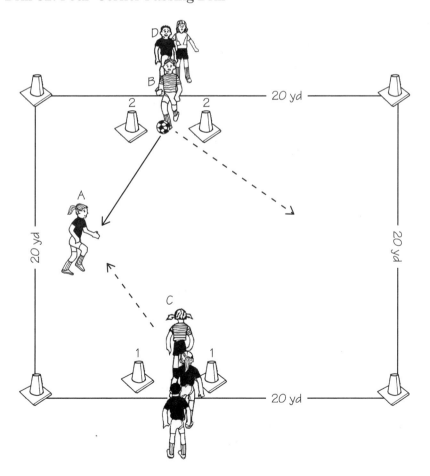

46   TWO-CONE DRILL

PURPOSE

To develop first-touch and passing accuracy with no defensive pressure.

LEVEL

Intermediate, advanced

EQUIPMENT

- 1 soccer ball
- 2 large game markers

TIME

10 minutes

PROCEDURE

1. Position two game markers 5 feet (1.5 m) apart.
2. Player A stands slightly behind and to the side of one of the markers, and player B, with the ball, stands 10 feet (3 m) in front of the middle of the markers (see figure).
3. Player A moves laterally from outside the first marker to a position between the two markers. In this position, he receives a pass and first-touches the ball to the outside of the second marker. He then passes the ball to player B.
4. Players repeat the action for one minute and then change roles.

KEY POINTS

Emphasize the importance of using the first touch to position the ball for the next play. A good first touch often means cushioning (i.e., slowing the pace of the ball by moving the contact foot slightly backward). A good first touch also allows the next play of the ball to occur quickly. Encourage players to use flat passes with correct pace on the ball. Variations of this drill might include having the receiver two-touch to the outside (i.e., touch the ball twice using one foot or a combination of the right and left feet), or having the receiver first-time the ball (i.e., pass the ball to a teammate on the first touch without collecting it).

TWO-CONE DRILL

46

RELATED DRILLS

Drill 35: Partner Passing Drill
Drill 50: Partner Thruway Drill
Drill 37: Thread-the-Needle Drill
Drill 43: Spaceman Drill
Drill 53: Pass-Dribble-Pass Drill
Drill 54: First-Touch Drill

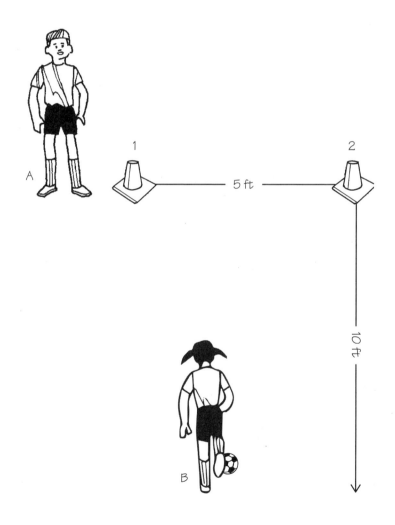

47 LINE DRILL

PURPOSE

To develop passing accuracy and collection skills from a moving player to a stationary target with no defensive pressure.

LEVEL

Intermediate

EQUIPMENT

1 soccer ball and 2 large game markers for every 3 players

TIME

5 minutes

PROCEDURE

1. Place two game markers 3 to 4 yards apart.
2. Position three players in a line (see figure).
3. Player B passes to player A, who collects, dribbles toward player C, and passes to player C.
4. Player C collects and dribbles toward player B, who has taken the place of player A.
5. Players repeat this action several times.

KEY POINTS

This is a fast-paced drill that provides opportunities for lots of touches on the ball. Encourage players to make collection as easy as possible by delivering flat, soft passes.

RELATED DRILLS

Drill 39: Good-Bye Drill
Drill 41: Circle Collection Drill
Drill 42: Hello Drill
Drill 44: Pendulum Drill
Drill 48: Two-Touch Drill
Drill 52: Four-Corner Passing Drill
Drill 45: Turning Drill

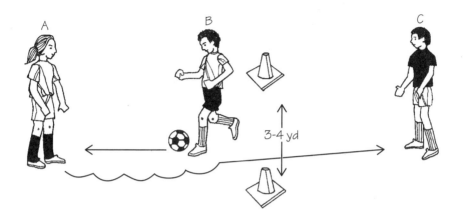

47

3-4 yd

TWO-TOUCH DRILL

PURPOSE

To develop passing accuracy and collection skills from a moving passer to a stationary target with no defensive pressure.

LEVEL

Advanced beginner, intermediate, advanced

EQUIPMENT

- 1 soccer ball
- 4 large game markers

TIME

10 minutes

PROCEDURE

1. Position players as shown in the figure.
2. On your signal, player A passes to player B. After passing the ball, player A switches lines and runs to a position behind player F.
3. Player B uses one touch to collect the pass from player A and another touch to push the ball away; then passes the ball to player C.
4. Player B continues running and assumes a position behind player E.
5. Players repeat the action.

KEY POINTS

As players' skills improve, so will their speed of play. It is essential that they collect and distribute the ball quickly as part of this transformation. Encourage players to cushion the ball while collecting. This keeps the ball in close proximity for the next touch. Challenge them to use flat passes with correct pacing to help receiving players collect passes more efficiently. You may want to make a game out of this drill by positioning two or more teams beside each other and challenging them to see which team can complete 20 passes first.

RELATED DRILLS

Drill 39: Good-Bye Drill

Drill 41: Circle Collection Drill

Drill 42: Hello Drill

Drill 44: Pendulum Drill

Drill 47: Line Drill

Drill 52: Four-Corner Passing Drill

Drill 45: Turning Drill

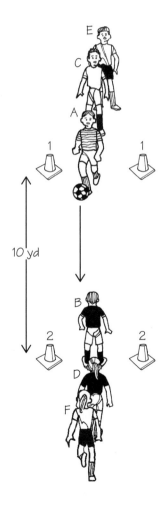

49 RETURN-TO-SENDER DRILL

PURPOSE

To develop passing accuracy and collection skills from a moving passer to a stationary target with no defensive pressure.

LEVEL

Intermediate, advanced

EQUIPMENT

- 1 soccer ball for every 2 players
- 4 large game markers
- 2 sets of jerseys (1 red set and 1 green set)—1 jersey for each player

TIME

10 minutes

PROCEDURE

1. Scatter players in a 30- by 30-yard grid (see figure).
2. Half the players wear red jerseys and the other half wear green.
3. The green players, each with a ball, move freely in the grid.
4. As a green player approaches a stationary red player, he passes to him, collects the return pass, moves through space again, and passes to another red player.
5. Green players move and pass for one minute, making as many passes as possible to different players.
6. Players reverse roles.
7. Vary this drill by having players pass at a variety of levels.

KEY POINTS

This drill goes more smoothly for beginning players when the stationary players collect the ball with their hands and then roll it back to the passers, who should be moving to a new space. As the players become more skillful, require them to collect with various body parts or to execute one-touch passes.

RETURN-TO-SENDER DRILL

49

RELATED DRILLS

Drill 36: Knockout Game

Drill 38: The Round-Up Game

Drill 51: Three-Player Passing Drill

Drill 40: Two-Team Passing Challenge Game

Drill 55: Three-Team Passing Drill

50 PARTNER THRUWAY DRILL

PURPOSE

To develop passing accuracy from a moving passer to a moving target with no defensive pressure.

LEVEL

Advanced beginner

EQUIPMENT

- 1 soccer ball for each set of partners
- 4 large game markers
- 12 small game markers

TIME

10 minutes

PROCEDURE

1. Position players in a 30- by 30-yard grid, as shown in the figure.
2. On your signal, players with the ball move to a space occupied by a set of game markers.
3. If the game markers are spaced 2 feet (0.6 m) apart, partners position themselves to make short passes to each other between the markers (i.e., no more than 3 yards). The partners then travel to a new set of game markers.
4. If the game markers are positioned 10 feet (3 m) apart, partners position themselves to make longer passes between the markers.
5. Players repeat the actions.

KEY POINTS

This is a fun activity that helps players develop good visual habits and communication. Emphasize the need to move to open spaces that are not occupied by other sets of partners. You may want to make a game of this drill. Challenge players to see which pair can pass through all the sets of markers first, or how many sets of markers they can negotiate in three minutes.

RELATED DRILLS

Drill 35: Partner Passing Drill

Drill 37: Thread-the-Needle Drill

Drill 43: Spaceman Drill

Drill 46: Two-Cone Drill

Drill 53: Pass-Dribble-Pass Drill

Drill 54: First-Touch Drill

51 THREE-PLAYER PASSING DRILL

PURPOSE

To develop passing combination play between teammates with no defensive pressure.

LEVEL

Advanced

EQUIPMENT

- 1 ball for every 3 players
- 4 large game markers

TIME

10 minutes

PROCEDURE

1. Scatter groups of three players in a 30- by 30-yard grid as shown in the figure.
2. On your signal, players move throughout the grid.
3. As the players move, they watch the positioning of the other players in their groups.
4. The player with the ball, player A, dribbles through open spaces while the other players in the group position for a pass.
5. One of the players without the ball, player B, moves to a space 3 to 5 yards from the dribbler to give close support. The other player without the ball, player C, moves farther away from player A to provide more width or depth for a pass.
6. As play continues, the roles of the players change. For example, if player A passes to player C, player B then gives close support, and player A provides width.

KEY POINTS

There are endless opportunities for combination play among the first attacker (the player with the ball), the second attacker (the teammate who is closer to the player with the ball), and the third attacker (the teammate providing width and depth). Encourage creative combination play while using good visual techniques to avoid passing and moving into closed space.

RELATED DRILLS

Drill 36: Knockout Game
Drill 38: The Round-Up Game
Drill 49: Return-to-Sender Drill
Drill 40: Two-Team Passing Challenge Game
Drill 55: Three-Team Passing Drill

52 FOUR-CORNER PASSING DRILL

PURPOSE

To develop passing accuracy and collection skills from a moving passer to a moving target with no defensive pressure.

LEVEL

Intermediate, advanced

EQUIPMENT

1 soccer ball and 4 large game markers for every 5 players

TIME

5 minutes

PROCEDURE

1. Position four players in the corners of a 10- by 10-yard grid (see figure).
2. Player E is outside the grid beside player A, ready to occupy that space when player A leaves.
3. Player A moves toward and passes to player B, who begins to move when player A reaches the halfway point between them.
4. After passing to player B, player A continues to move and occupies player B's original space.
5. Player B collects on the move and passes to player C, who begins to move when player B reaches the halfway point between them.
6. Players continue this action of collecting while moving, passing to the next player, and then occupying that player's corner of the grid.
7. As passing skills improve, challenge players by counting how many times they can pass the ball around the entire grid in two minutes.

KEY POINTS

Passers should make eye contact with the players they are passing to and should lead them with a pass that they can easily collect.

You may use more players in this drill by positioning them by the corners outside the grid. As a player completes the pass, she goes to the end of the line instead of standing by the marker.

RELATED DRILLS

Drill 39: Good-Bye Drill
Drill 41: Circle Collection Drill
Drill 42: Hello Drill
Drill 44: Pendulum Drill
Drill 47: Line Drill
Drill 48: Two-Touch Drill
Drill 45: Turning Drill

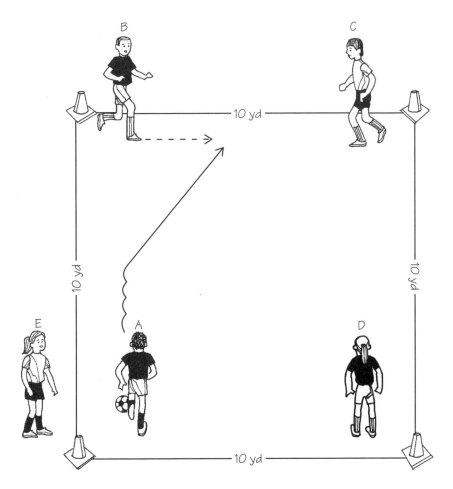

PASS-DRIBBLE-PASS DRILL

PURPOSE

To develop passing accuracy and collection skills from a moving passer to a moving target with no defensive pressure.

LEVEL

Intermediate, advanced

EQUIPMENT

1 soccer ball and 4 large game markers for every 2 players

TIME

5 minutes

PROCEDURE

Level 1

1. Position two players in a 15- by 15-yard grid (see figure).
2. Player A passes to player B, who dribbles into open space, turns, and then passes back to player A, who has moved to a new space behind her.
3. Players repeat this action.

Level 2

1. Remove game markers.
2. Players repeat the action while moving in general space.

KEY POINTS

This drill requires players to pass the ball backward. Players who position themselves behind another player should communicate that they are in an open space by saying "Drop." Players who pass backward should practice using the heel to pass and changing the position of the body in relation to the ball, as demonstrated in the step-over move. At level 2, encourage partners to communicate with each other so that they do not become separated when moving among other partner groups in general space.

PASS-DRIBBLE-PASS DRILL 53

RELATED DRILLS

Drill 35: Partner Passing Drill

Drill 50: Partner Thruway Drill

Drill 37: Thread-the-Needle Drill

Drill 43: Spaceman Drill

Drill 46: Two-Cone Drill

Drill 54: First-Touch Drill

54 FIRST-TOUCH DRILL

PURPOSE

To develop passing accuracy from a moving passer to a moving target with no defensive pressure.

LEVEL

Advanced

EQUIPMENT

- 1 soccer ball for every 2 players
- 4 large game markers

TIME

5 minutes

PROCEDURE

1. Players scatter in pairs within a 20- by 20-yard grid.
2. Each set of partners has a ball (see figure).
3. On your signal, the players begin to move through the grid.
4. The players with the balls pass to their partners, who must pass back on the first touch.
5. Partners continue moving, using only one-touch passing.

KEY POINTS

Players must use good visual techniques to negotiate space and avoid other players. Initially, partners should move with no more than 4 yards between them. As they become more proficient at one-touch passing, they can be farther apart.

RELATED DRILLS

Drill 35: Partner Passing Drill
Drill 50: Partner Thruway Drill
Drill 37: Thread-the-Needle Drill
Drill 43: Spaceman Drill
Drill 46: Two-Cone Drill
Drill 53: Pass-Dribble-Pass Drill

55 THREE-TEAM PASSING DRILL

PURPOSE

To develop passing accuracy with no defensive pressure.

LEVEL

Intermediate, advanced

EQUIPMENT

- 3 soccer balls
- 4 large game markers
- 12 jerseys (4 red, 4 blue, 4 green)

TIME

10 minutes

PROCEDURE

1. Position four game markers to make a 30- by 30-yard grid.
2. Twelve players divided into three teams (red, blue, and green) scatter in the grid, four players per team (see figure). One player from each team has a ball.
3. On your signal, players move throughout the grid passing to teammates.

KEY POINTS

Encourage players to move to open spaces to support the player with the ball and to communicate with their teammates. Good visual scanning will enable players to find the open spaces. Variations of this drill include numbering players on each team to pass consecutively (number 1 passes to number 2, and so forth), requiring players to pass between two like opponents (two red players, two blue players), restricting the number of touches (two touches, one touch), and using two balls for each team. Encourage players to use the entire width and depth of the grid as they move. Note that teams do not play defense during this drill.

RELATED DRILLS

Drill 36: Knockout Game

Drill 38: The Round-Up Game

Drill 51: Three-Player Passing Drill

Drill 49: Return-to-Sender Drill

Drill 40: Two-Team Passing Challenge Game

56   INVISIBLE MAN DRILL

PURPOSE

To develop passing and collecting skills with subtle defensive pressure.

LEVEL

Intermediate, advanced

EQUIPMENT

1 soccer ball and 4 large game markers for every 3 players

TIME

5 minutes

PROCEDURE

1. Position three players in a 10- by 10-yard grid.
2. Players are in a straight line, with players B and C looking in the direction of player A, who has the ball (see figure).
3. Player B, the defender, can move laterally but not forward or backward.
4. Player C moves either right or left to receive a pass from player A.
5. Player B then faces player C, and players repeat the action.
6. After several rounds, have players change roles.

KEY POINTS

Adding a defender (player B) subtly pressures the passer, because the defender blocks her vision. In fact, if player C does not move into open space, she is practically invisible to player A.

RELATED DRILLS

Drill 57: Star Drill
Drill 58: Monkey-in-the-Middle Drill
Drill 60: Keep-Away Drill

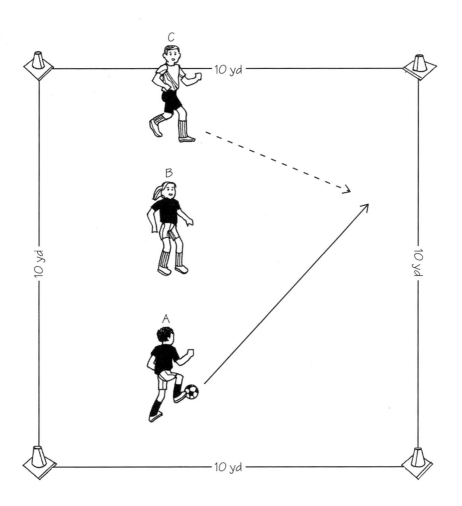

57 STAR DRILL

PURPOSE

To develop passing and collecting skills with subtle defensive pressure.

LEVEL

Intermediate, advanced

EQUIPMENT

1 soccer ball for every 6 players

TIME

5 minutes

PROCEDURE

1. Position five players to form the five points of a star (see figure).
2. Place one defender in the middle of the star.
3. Players try to make as many consecutive passes as possible without losing control or allowing the defender to touch the ball.
4. Players may not pass the ball to the players beside them.

KEY POINTS

This is a 5v1 drill in which the offensive players have a big advantage. Beginning players need this advantage to have enough time to collect the ball, look around, and decide where and how to pass it.

RELATED DRILLS

Drill 56: Invisible Man Drill
Drill 58: Monkey-in-the-Middle Drill
Drill 60: Keep-Away Drill

58 MONKEY-IN-THE-MIDDLE DRILL

PURPOSE

To develop passing and collecting skills with subtle pressure and practice moving without the ball and making decisions concerning the use of open and closed space.

LEVEL

Advanced beginner, intermediate

EQUIPMENT

1 soccer ball and 4 large game markers for every 4 players

TIME

10 minutes

PROCEDURE

1. Position four game markers to make a 10- by 10-yard grid. Three players stand by three of the markers.
2. A fourth player is in the middle and is affectionately referred to as the "monkey" (see figure).
3. This is a 3v1 keep-away game.
4. Players on the perimeter may not pass the ball across the middle of the square. This limitation forces players to move constantly to support positions so that the passer always has two passing lanes from which to choose.
5. If the player by game marker 1 has the ball, the other two players move to spaces by game markers 2 and 4.
6. If the player in the middle (the defender) closes the space between game markers 1 and 2, then the pass is made to the player at game marker 4.
7. The receiving players then move to game markers 1 and 3.
8. Because a player already occupies game marker 1, the player who was at game marker 2 moves to game marker 3 to support the passer.
9. It is impossible for the defender to close both passing lanes.
10. The defender earns his way out of the middle by touching the ball or forcing an error in passing or collecting.

MONKEY-IN-THE-MIDDLE DRILL 58

KEY POINTS

Perimeter players must collect the ball, look around, and decide among passing choices. They also must communicate with each other concerning space. Variations of this drill include limiting touches on the ball, allowing players to use diagonal runs to space, and allowing dribbling to space.

RELATED DRILLS

Drill 56: Invisible Man Drill
Drill 57: Star Drill
Drill 60: Keep-Away Drill

59   LONG BALL DRILL

PURPOSE

To develop long- and short-passing skills with subtle defensive pressure.

LEVEL

Advanced

EQUIPMENT

- 2 soccer balls
- 2 scrimmage jerseys
- 16 large game markers

TIME

15 minutes

PROCEDURE

1. Position players in four grids as shown in the figure.
2. On your signal, players in grids 1 and 3 play a 5v1 keep-away game. One player, identified by holding a scrimmage jersey, is the defender.
3. After the fourth pass in grids 1 and 3, the player collecting the ball must pass it to a grid occupied by only one player (grid 2 or 4). All the players follow the ball to the next grid except the player who passed the ball.
4. If the defender (the player holding the scrimmage jersey) can steal the ball or cause the ball to be played outside the grid before the fifth pass, she gives her scrimmage jersey to the player who made mistake (who is now the new defender) and becomes part of the passing team. When a passer becomes the defender, the drill begins again; the passers have to make four consecutive passes before passing the ball and moving to another grid.

KEY POINTS

Encourage players to make short passes that are easy to collect when passing in the grid and long passes with accuracy when passing outside the grid. Challenge them to look carefully before decid-ing which grid to play to next. If making four consecutive passes is too difficult for players, reduce the number of passes needed to play the ball to the next grid or increase the size of the grid. If play-ers are not challenged enough, reduce the size of the grid or add another defender.

RELATED DRILL

Drill 61: Three-Team Keep-Away Game

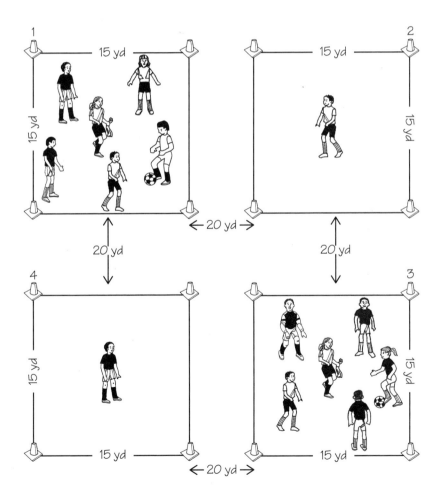

60   KEEP-AWAY DRILL

PURPOSE

To develop the techniques and tactics used by the second attacker.

LEVEL

Intermediate, advanced

EQUIPMENT

- 1 ball
- 4 large game markers
- 1 red jersey

TIME

10 minutes

PROCEDURE

1. Position four game markers to make a 20- by 20-yard grid.
2. Three players are positioned inside the grid—two offensive players and one defensive player in the red jersey (see figure).
3. On your signal, the two offensive players try to maintain possession of the ball while the player with the red jersey defends.
4. After one minute, or if the defender either gains possession or causes the ball to be played outside the grid, have players switch roles.

KEY POINTS

Initially, players who assume the role of the second attacker tend to run away from the ball, attempting to move as far away from the defender as possible. Teach players instead to assume a position of close support (the role of the second attacker), which will enable them to work with the first attacker to confuse the defender. Encourage the use of the wall pass, the takeover, and the overlap pass. For a wall pass, the second attacker receives a short pass, immediately executes another short pass behind the defender and close to the first attacker, collects the ball, and continues to run. When executing a takeover, the second attacker runs behind and close to the first attacker, collects the ball, and continues to run. In the overlap pass, the second attacker runs behind the first attacker and continues a curved run forward at an angle wide enough to receive a pass.

Variations of this drill include adding a server outside of the grid to initiate action by serving the ball on the ground or in the air, or by throwing the ball in. You can also change the drill by restricting the number of touches on the ball by the offensive players (e.g., two touches). Or you can add more structure, requiring the two offensive players to move the ball from one endline to the other under a time constraint (e.g., 20 seconds).

RELATED DRILLS

Drill 56: Invisible Man Drill
Drill 57: Star Drill
Drill 58: Monkey-in-the-Middle Drill

61 THREE-TEAM KEEP-AWAY GAME

PURPOSE

To develop passing accuracy under subtle defensive pressure.

LEVEL

Advanced

EQUIPMENT

- 1 soccer ball
- 4 large game markers
- 9 jerseys (3 red, 3 yellow, 3 blue)

TIME

10 minutes

PROCEDURE

1. Position four game markers to make a 30- by 30-yard square.
2. Divide nine players into three teams of three players wearing the same color jerseys (see figure).
3. The red and blue teams begin passing to each other while keeping the ball away from the yellow team. Each time they are successful passing to a red or blue team member they earn 1 point. The yellow team plays defense, trying to recover possession of the ball.
4. If the yellow team gains possession or the ball is played outside the grid, the team that made the mistake must now play defense and is penalized 1 point.
5. If the red team is on defense, the yellow team combines with the blue team to keep the ball away from the red team. Each time they are successful passing to a yellow or blue team member they earn 1 point.
6. Each time a team has to play defense, it is penalized 1 point.
7. At the end of 10 minutes, the team with the most points is declared the winner.
8. The action is repeated: two teams pass the ball while keeping it away from the third team.

KEY POINTS

This activity offers a numbers advantage (more players) for the two teams in possession of the ball. This advantage increases the likelihood of connecting passes between players. To help players become more successful in keeping the ball away from opponents, encourage them to use good visual scanning techniques. This will help them see players in open spaces to whom they may pass. Emphasize to players without the ball that movement to open spaces creates passing opportunities. Encourage the second attacker (teammate closest to the player with the ball) to provide close support and the third attackers (all teammates who are not the first and second attackers) to provide width, depth, and mobility.

RELATED DRILL

Drill 59: Long Ball Drill

62

CONE DRILL

PURPOSE

To develop passing and collecting skills with gamelike defensive pressure.

LEVEL

Intermediate, advanced

EQUIPMENT

1 soccer ball and 5 large game markers for every 6 players

TIME

10 minutes

PROCEDURE

1. Position a player on each side of a 15- by 15-yard grid.
2. One of these players has a ball.
3. Place a game marker in the center of the grid.
4. Two players are inside the grid (see figure). One is an offensive player, and the other is a defensive player.
5. The offensive player must run around the cone and sprint toward the player with the ball.
6. The player with the ball passes to the offensive player if she is in an open space.
7. If the defender closes the space, the passer instead passes to another player on the grid.
8. The offensive player repeats, going around the cone toward the new player with the ball.
9. The offensive player collects and returns the ball each time to the passer, who then passes to another player on the perimeter of the grid.

KEY POINTS

Challenge players to count how many times the offensive player receives a pass in one minute. Passers must give the offensive players soft passes to collect. Defensive players work hard to close the space between the offensive player and the passer. Increase the difficulty of collection for more advanced players by having them serve balls at various speeds and levels.

RELATED DRILLS

Drill 63: Check Out–Check In Drill
Drill 64: 1v1 Drill
Drill 65: 2v2 Keep-Away Drill
Drill 67: 3v2 Line Game

63 CHECK OUT–CHECK IN DRILL

PURPOSE

To develop passing and collecting skills under gamelike defensive pressure.

LEVEL

Intermediate, advanced

EQUIPMENT

1 soccer ball and 4 large game markers for every 6 players

TIME

10 minutes

PROCEDURE

1. Position a player on each side of a 15- by 15-yard grid.
2. One player has the ball.
3. Two players (A and B) are inside the grid (see figure).
4. Player A runs away (checks out) from the ball, changes direction, and then sprints toward the ball (checks in) to receive a pass.
5. If the defender (player B) closes the space, the passer plays the ball to another player on the grid.
6. If the offensive player collects the pass, she shields the ball for 5 to 10 seconds before returning a pass to anyone on the grid.
7. Challenge players to count how many consecutive passes the offensive player receives in one minute without the defensive player touching the ball.

KEY POINTS

Offensive players should move away from the ball at a moderate speed. After changing direction, they should accelerate toward the ball. Changing speed makes denying space more difficult for the defender.

CHECK OUT–CHECK IN DRILL

RELATED DRILLS

Drill 62: Cone Drill
Drill 64: 1v1 Drill
Drill 65: 2v2 Keep-Away Drill
Drill 67: 3v2 Line Game

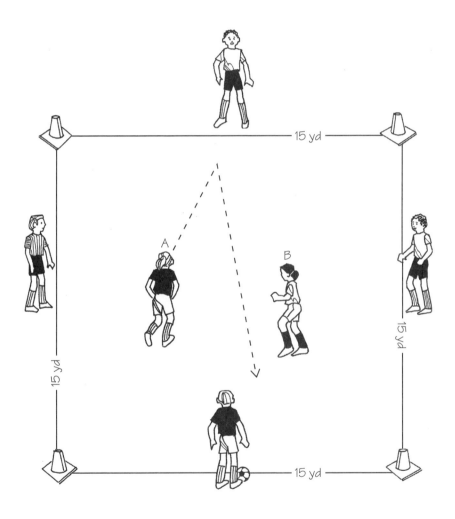

64   1v1 DRILL

PURPOSE

To develop decision-making abilities concerning passing choices under gamelike defensive pressure.

LEVEL

Intermediate, advanced

EQUIPMENT

- 1 soccer ball
- 1 jersey for the defender
- 2 jerseys (different color from defender jersey) for neutral players
- 4 large game markers for every 4 players

TIME

10 minutes

PROCEDURE

Level 1

1. Position four players in a 15- by 15-yard grid—one offensive, one defensive, and two neutral players (see figure).
2. The offensive player passes to one of the neutral players and then moves to open space to receive a return pass.
3. Players try to connect as many consecutive passes as possible.
4. If the defender gains possession, she becomes the offensive player.
5. After one minute of possession, have the neutral players switch roles with the offensive and defensive players.

Level 2

1. Follow level 1 procedures, but use only one neutral player.
2. Apply a two-touch limit.

1v1 DRILL

KEY POINTS

Players must quickly change speed and direction to create space for passes. Variations of this drill include adding players to make the drill 2v2 or 3v3. Add goals to encourage finishing skills. Neutral players may not be defended against.

RELATED DRILLS

Drill 62: Cone Drill
Drill 63: Check Out–Check In Drill
Drill 60: 2v2 Keep-Away Drill
Drill 67: 3v2 Line Game

65   2v2 KEEP-AWAY DRILL

PURPOSE

To develop the techniques and tactics used by the second attacker.

LEVEL

Intermediate, advanced

EQUIPMENT

- 1 ball
- 4 large game markers
- 4 jerseys (2 blue, 2 red)

TIME

10 minutes

PROCEDURE

1. Position four game markers to make a 20- by 20-yard grid.
2. Four players are in the grid, two red and two blue (see figure).
3. On your signal, the two offensive players try to keep the ball away from the two defensive players.
4. After one minute, or if the defensive players gain possession of the ball or cause it to be played outside the grid, players switch roles.

KEY POINTS

Encourage offensive players to confuse the defenders with creative moves by the second attacker, who can provide opportunities for ball passes, takeovers, and overlaps. Vary the drill by requiring the team in possession of the ball to move from one end of the grid to the other within a time restriction (such as 30 seconds). This drill also develops the roles of the first defender (who defends against the player with the ball, denying penetration) and the second defender (who defends against the offensive teammate closer to the player with the ball, providing cover for the first defender). Use this drill as either an offensive or a defensive instruction tool, but do not confuse players by commenting on both aspects of play at the same time.

RELATED DRILLS

Drill 62: Cone Drill
Drill 63: Check Out–Check In Drill
Drill 64: 1v1 Drill
Drill 67: 3v2 Line Game

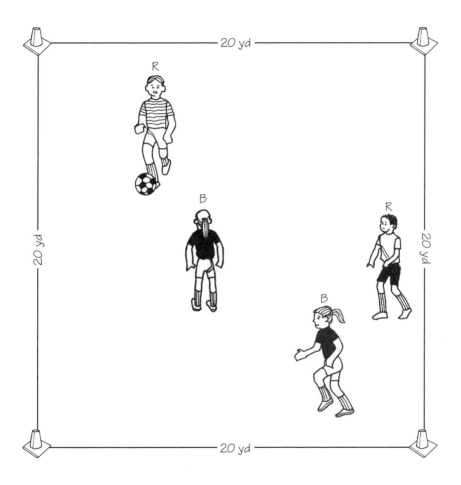

66 TWO-TEAMMATE PASSING GAME

PURPOSE

To develop the techniques and tactics used by the second attacker.

LEVEL

Intermediate, advanced

EQUIPMENT

- 1 ball
- 4 large game markers
- 12 jerseys (6 red, 6 blue)

TIME

20 minutes

PROCEDURE

1. Position four game markers to make a 20- by 30-yard grid.
2. Inside the grid, position two red and two blue players. One team starts with the ball.
3. Position one red and one blue player on each 20-yard endline and each 30-yard side of the grid (see figure).
4. On your whistle, the team in possession of the ball tries to pass the ball to a teammate on either end of the grid.
5. The end player passes the ball back to a teammate inside the grid.
6. Teammates inside the grid then pass the ball to the teammate on the opposite end.
7. Each pass to one end player and then the other, maintaining possession of the ball, results in 1 point for that team.
8. After three minutes, inside players rotate to the side, side players to the end, and end players to the inside of the grid.
9. Players repeat the action.

KEY POINTS

This is a passing drill, so limit players to three touches on the ball. Encourage the inside players to make quick give-and-go passes to their teammates on the sides. Also, remind the inside players that the second attacker works with the first attacker (the one with the ball) to penetrate the defense. Review the positioning and movements of the second attacker. He should stay close enough to work with the first attacker using short passes, but far enough away that one defender cannot successfully defend against both players. Remind players that this sort of teamwork allows creative plays such as wall passes, takeovers, and overlaps. Sideline and endline players do not defend each other.

RELATED DRILL

Drill 68: Two-Team Keep-Away Game

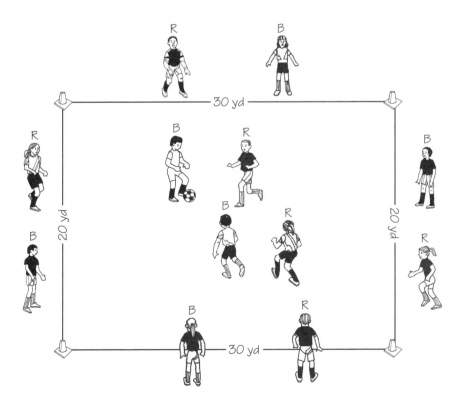

67   3v2 LINE GAME

PURPOSE

To develop the techniques and tactics used by the third attacker.

LEVEL

Intermediate, advanced

EQUIPMENT

- 1 ball
- 4 large game markers
- 6 jerseys (3 red, 3 blue)

TIME

10 minutes

PROCEDURE

1. Position four game markers to make a 20- by 40-yard grid.
2. Position three offensive players (red) and two defensive players (blue) inside the grid. A third blue player is positioned outside of the grid by side 2 (see figure).
3. On your signal, the three red players try to keep the ball in their possession while moving it from side 1 to side 2 of the grid. If they cross the line on side 2, they earn 1 point.
4. If the members of the red team are successful, or if they lose possession of the ball, one of them must go outside of the grid by side 1. The third blue player then enters from side 2. The blue team now tries to move the ball from side 2 to side 1. If they cross the line on side 1, they earn 1 point.
5. Play continues until one of the teams scores 10 points.

KEY POINTS

This drill enables players to develop the role of the third attacker, which is to create space to receive the ball behind the defenders. Encourage the player who is not being defended against to make wide, bending runs to attract the defenders' attention and cause confusion. Restrict touches on the ball by the offensive team at first, which will necessitate less dribbling and more passing.

3v2 LINE GAME 67

RELATED DRILLS

Drill 62: Cone Drill

Drill 63: Check Out–Check In Drill

Drill 64: 1v1 Drill

Drill 65: 2v2 Keep-Away Drill

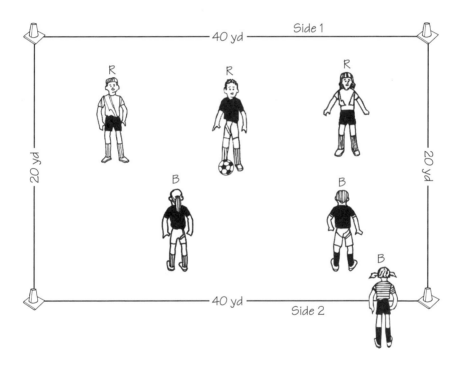

68 TWO-TEAM KEEP-AWAY GAME

PURPOSE

To develop passing accuracy with gamelike defensive pressure.

LEVEL

Intermediate, advanced

EQUIPMENT

- 1 ball
- 6 large game markers
- 8 jerseys (4 blue, 4 red)

TIME

10 minutes

PROCEDURE

1. Position six game markers to make two 20- by 20-yard grids side by side.
2. Four blue players scatter in grid 1. One player has a ball (see figure).
3. The four red players scatter in grid 2.
4. On your signal, the blue team tries to connect as many passes as possible. Every time they connect five passes in a row, they earn 1 point.
5. On your signal to begin play, the red team sends two players (defenders) into grid 1.
6. If the red players touch the ball or cause it to be played outside the grid, the red team gains possession of the ball.
7. The red defender closest to the ball is then allowed one free pass to a teammate in grid 2. Blue players must freeze until the ball is played to grid 2, at which time they may send two defenders into grid 2 to try to prevent the red team from connecting passes.
8. Players repeat the procedure.
9. The team that scores 5 points first is declared the winner.

TWO-TEAM KEEP-AWAY GAME

68

KEY POINTS

This is a tactical (decision-making) exercise using passing techniques. Encourage players to use vision, communication, and movement to keep the ball away from their opponents. Emphasize the importance of spacing players across the depth and width of the grid. Limit dribbling initially to three touches on the ball. As players develop their skills, impose a no-dribble rule.

RELATED DRILL

Drill 66: Two-Teammate Passing Game

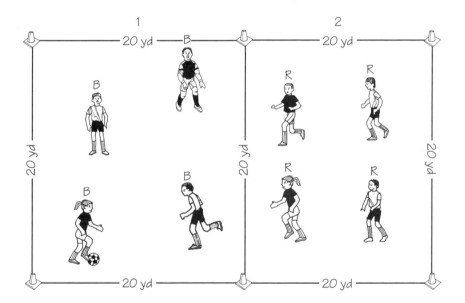

4

Heading Drills

Heading is a method of controlling the ball to pass or shoot and is generally regarded as one of the most difficult soccer skills to master. There is some controversy among coaches and medical personnel about when the teaching of heading progressions should begin. Regardless of your stance on this issue, when you initiate the process, you can put certain procedures into place to ensure that your players are in the safest learning environment possible. Teaching proper heading techniques using a developmental process and age-appropriate equipment and having officials that enforce the rules of heading all contribute to a safer learning environment.

When players begin learning how to head a ball, they mostly fear being struck in the face with a ball. When teaching heading skills, you can address this concern by using a sponge-type ball. In some cases it may be necessary to use a slightly larger and lighter ball (similar to a beach ball) to reduce players' fears. The teaching progression for heading is as follows:

1. No defensive pressure, tossing softly to self from knees
2. Standing and tossing to self
3. Standing with partner tossing
4. Heading with subtle defensive pressure
5. Heading with gamelike defensive pressure

Begin the heading progression by positioning players on their knees to ensure proper balance of the lower body. Challenge them to keep their eyes open and watch the ball as they strike it using the part of the head commonly referred to as the forehead. While they are on their knees with eyes open and mouths closed, encourage players to concentrate on the action of their upper bodies. As they begin to feel more comfortable striking the ball with their heads, they can move to a standing position. At this stage players begin to learn about the contributions the lower body makes to heading.

For the next step in the progression, partners toss the ball to each other while stationary and then while in motion. Emphasize positioning the body to get under the ball at this level. As players gain more confidence, have them jump and head the ball using a one-foot takeoff. During this process, encourage them to keep their mouths closed to avoid injury to their tongues, and to keep their eyes open so they can track the pathway of the ball. Tracking the pathway of the ball allows them to strike the ball more intentionally instead of letting the ball strike them, which will be helpful later in the progression when they are learning to redirect the ball toward a teammate or goal. The intended pathway of the ball determines what part of the ball the player should apply force to and how much force other body parts should generate. For example, a player who wants to head the ball toward the ground strikes the ball with a downward motion of the forehead. To send the ball upward, she strikes the bottom portion of the ball with the forehead. To make the ball travel to the right, the player can maneuver her body before the ball arrives to strike it in that direction.

The amount of force a player should use on the ball is determined by how far the ball must travel after contact. A player generates force by bending at the waist and snapping the head and shoulders forward.

The position of the ball in relation to the player and the position of the player on the field are other factors that determine proper heading techniques. Players in the defensive third of the field generally head the ball high and wide, away from their goal. Players in the midfield should play the ball more precisely, because they are often trying to head it to teammates who are attacking players. Players in the offensive third of the field use heading skills mainly for scoring opportunities. Placement, not power, is essential for these players.

Challenge your players by offering heading drills with subtle and gamelike defensive pressure. Refining heading skills is another step toward adding more structure to the game and developing intentional play.

69 TOSS-TO-SELF HEADING DRILL

PURPOSE

To develop the skill of striking the ball with the part of the forehead known as the hairline, with no defensive pressure.

LEVEL

Beginner, advanced beginner

EQUIPMENT

1 foam ball or beach ball for every player

TIME

5 minutes

PROCEDURE

Level 1

1. Position players in a scattered formation.
2. Players should be on their knees, each with a ball. Players toss the ball slightly above their heads (see figure), strike it gently with their heads, and then catch it before it hits the ground.
3. Players repeat this several times.

Level 2

After players have demonstrated correct heading techniques, have them repeat the level 1 steps while standing.

KEY POINTS

Show players the location of the hairline. Emphasize moving the head to strike the ball instead of merely positioning the head so the ball hits it. Insist that players strike the ball with their eyes open and mouths closed. This will prevent them from biting their tongues later when using a harder ball. At level 2, encourage players to establish a good base of support by flexing their knees slightly and positioning their feet a little more than shoulder-width apart.

RELATED DRILLS

Drill 70: Partner Heading Drill
Drill 71: Sliding Heading Drill

70   PARTNER HEADING DRILL

PURPOSE

To develop proper heading technique with no defensive pressure.

LEVEL

Beginner, advanced beginner

EQUIPMENT

- 1 foam, sponge, or beach ball for every 2 players
- 4 large game markers

TIME

5 minutes

PROCEDURE

Level 1

1. Position partners in a 30- by 30-yard grid (see figure).
2. Each pair of players has a ball.
3. The player with the ball tosses to himself and heads the ball to his partner, who catches, tosses, and heads it back.

Level 2

1. Players should be about 5 yards apart during this level of the drill.
2. Instead of tossing to himself, the player tosses to his partner, who returns the ball by heading.
3. Gradually increase the distance between partners as both tossing and heading skills improve.

Level 3

1. One partner tosses to the other partner, who is in motion. The player in motion returns the ball by heading.
2. The player in motion should change direction—forward, backward, left, and right.

KEY POINTS

Partners should select a type of ball with which they feel comfortable. Teach them to generate more force by bending backward at the waist and then thrusting forward to contact the ball. Players should flex their knees and extend their arms to improve balance.

RELATED DRILLS

Drill 69: Toss-to-Self Heading Drill
Drill 71: Sliding Heading Drill

71 SLIDING HEADING DRILL

PURPOSE

To develop heading technique while in motion with no defensive pressure.

LEVEL

Intermediate, advanced

EQUIPMENT

- 1 soccer ball
- 4 large game markers

TIME

5 minutes

PROCEDURE

1. Position two players on opposite sides of a 5- by 20-yard grid as shown in the figure.
2. Player A slides from game marker 1 to game marker 2, while player B slides from game marker 3 to game marker 4.
3. While sliding, player B tosses the ball to player A, who returns it by heading.
4. When the players reach the end of the grid, they reverse roles.

KEY POINTS

Heading while in motion is difficult for players to master but is an essential part of the game. Encourage players to control the direction of the ball by striking it with the upper part of the forehead. Challenge them to keep their eyes open and follow the path of the ball until impacting it with the head.

RELATED DRILLS

Drill 69: Toss-to-Self Heading Drill
Drill 70: Partner Heading Drill

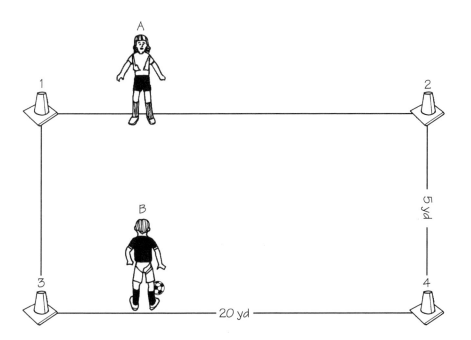

72 SHORT AND LONG HEADING DRILL

PURPOSE

To develop force relationships when heading with no defensive pressure.

LEVEL

Intermediate, advanced

EQUIPMENT

2 soccer balls and 4 large game markers for every 3 players

TIME

5 minutes

PROCEDURE

Level 1

1. Position three players in a 10- by 10-yard grid.
2. Players B and C each have a ball (see figure).
3. Player B takes a position 5 yards from player A, and player C takes a position 10 yards from player A. Player B tosses to player A, who returns the ball by heading. Then player C tosses his ball to player A, and player A repeats the heading action.

Level 2

1. After the first toss, only heading skills may be used to pass the ball.
2. Player B tosses to player A.
3. Player A heads to player C.
4. Player C heads to player A, who returns the ball by heading to player B.
5. Players repeat this action.

KEY POINTS

Players need to learn to generate different amounts of force because of the various distances the ball must travel. Emphasize that the speed with which the head strikes the ball is the major factor in generating this force. Players can increase head speed by bending at the waist and thrusting the upper body forward. Encourage them to move their feet to get into good positions for striking the ball.

RELATED DRILLS

Drill 74: Star Heading Drill
Drill 75: Three-Corner Heading Drill

73 TWO-TEAM HEADING GAME

PURPOSE

To develop passing accuracy using heading skills with no defensive pressure.

LEVEL

Advanced

EQUIPMENT

- 2 soccer balls
- 16 large game markers

TIME

10 minutes

PROCEDURE

1. Position two teams of four players as shown in the figure.
2. On your signal, the first player on each team tosses the ball to the player in grid 1. For example, player A tosses the ball to player B. Player B heads the ball back to player A.
3. Player A then tosses to player C, who heads the ball back to player A.
4. Player A then tosses to player D, who heads the ball back to player A.
5. If everyone is successful, player A moves to grid 1, player B moves to grid 2, player C moves to grid 3, and player D replaces player A in front of the grids.
6. If during the action a player does not head the ball back to the tosser so it can be caught in the air, the tosser must try again by serving a second ball to that player. After three unsuccessful attempts, the tosser moves on to the next player.
7. The game continues until all players rotate back to their starting positions. The first team to return to their starting position is declared the winner.

KEY POINTS

Make grids approximately 10 yards wide and 5 yards deep. Ten-yard-wide grids provide players with plenty of space for executing the heading skill. Making the grids only 5 yards deep reduces the length of the toss, which should help with tossing accuracy. It also reduces the length of the return by the player heading the ball. When they are heading balls longer distances, challenge your players to arch their backs and bring their heads and shoulders forward to impact the ball. This motion creates more force and carries the ball farther.

RELATED DRILLS

None

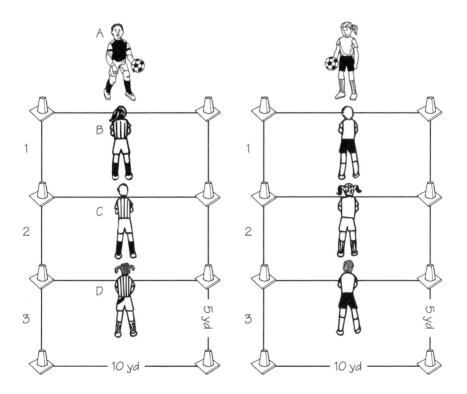

74   STAR HEADING DRILL

PURPOSE

To improve the heading skills used to change ball direction, with no defensive pressure at level 1 and with subtle defensive pressure at level 2.

LEVEL

Intermediate, advanced

EQUIPMENT

1 soccer ball and 1 large game marker for every 5 players

TIME

5 minutes

PROCEDURE

Level 1

1. Position players in a star formation, approximately 7 to 10 yards apart. One player has a ball.
2. Place a game marker in the middle of the star (see figure).
3. The player with the ball calls another player's name, and that player must run around the marker and head the tossed ball to another player.
4. Players continue this action.

Level 2

1. Players repeat level 1, steps 1 through 4.
2. Add a player in the middle of the star to provide subtle defensive pressure.

KEY POINTS

Encourage players to jump before striking the ball. Insist that they head the ball forward, backward, left, and right. The defensive player should be passive and not challenge in the air for the ball.

RELATED DRILLS

Drill 72: Short and Long Heading Drill
Drill 75: Three-Corner Heading Drill

75 THREE-CORNER HEADING DRILL

PURPOSE

To improve the heading skills used to change ball direction, with no defensive pressure at level 1 and subtle defensive pressure at level 2.

LEVEL

Intermediate, advanced

EQUIPMENT

1 soccer ball and 4 large game markers for every 3 players

TIME

5 minutes

PROCEDURE

Level 1

1. Position three players on the corners of a 10- by 10-yard grid (see figure).
2. Player A tosses the ball to player B.
3. Player B heads the ball to player C, who has moved to the open corner of the grid.
4. After player A tosses, she moves to the corner originally occupied by player C.
5. Player C tosses to player A, who heads the ball to moving player B, who has moved to the corner originally occupied by player A.
6. Players repeat this cycle several times.

Level 2

1. Players repeat level 1, steps 1 through 5.
2. Add defenders on the outside of the grid

KEY POINTS

Emphasize that players should lead their teammates by heading the ball to a location slightly in front of them, the same as they do when passing with the feet. Adding defending players on the outside of the grid encourages more precision with tosses and heading passes. Defenders are not allowed inside the grid and should subtly challenge in the air for head balls.

RELATED DRILLS

Drill 72: Short and Long Heading Drill
Drill 74: Star Heading Drill

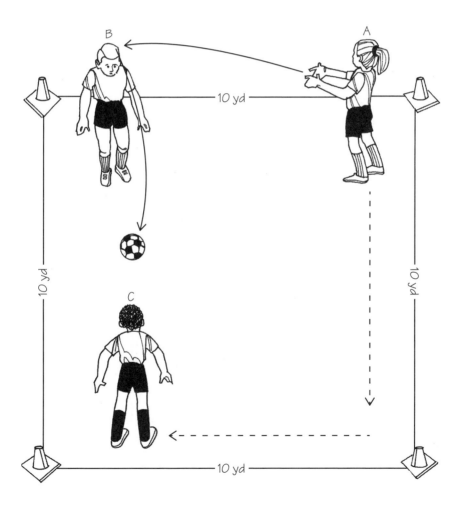

76   JACK-IN-THE-BOX DRILL

PURPOSE

To improve heading skills under subtle defensive pressure.

LEVEL

Advanced

EQUIPMENT

1 soccer ball and 2 large game markers for every 3 players

TIME

5 minutes

PROCEDURE

1. Position three players in a line.
2. Players A and C are approximately 10 yards apart; player B is halfway between them (see figure).
3. Player A tosses over player B to player C, who returns the ball by heading.
4. Players repeat several times and then change roles.

KEY POINTS

Player B provides subtle defensive pressure by obstructing the vision of player C. To add more defensive pressure, have player B jump as the ball is tossed. As the players' skills improve, reduce the distance between players B and C, and increase the distance between players A and C. Game markers help provide proper spacing so players do not drift too far apart.

RELATED DRILLS

None

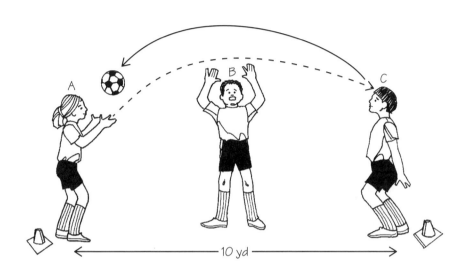

77   SHOW-FOR-ME DRILL

PURPOSE

To develop heading skills under gamelike defensive pressure.

LEVEL

Advanced

EQUIPMENT

1 soccer ball and 4 large game markers for every 3 players

TIME

5 minutes

PROCEDURE

1. Position three players in a 10- by 10-yard grid (see figure).
2. Player B runs away from the ball, then quickly changes speed and direction, coming back toward the ball.
3. Player A tosses the ball for player B to return by heading.
4. Player C challenges player B for the tossed ball.

KEY POINTS

Player C must not take a ball-side position on the initial run by player B. Encourage player C to move to a ball-side position and make the first touch only after player B changes direction and moves toward the ball.

RELATED DRILLS

None

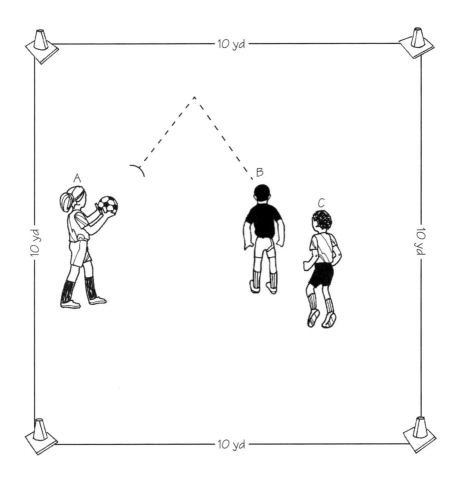

5

Shooting Drills

Because young players have the most fun when they are scoring goals, practice sessions should include lots of opportunities for them to practice scoring. You can make these opportunities available during full-field scrimmages, small-sided games, and shooting drills. During full-field and small-sided games, vary procedures to encourage more goal scoring. Include games with no goalkeepers, or restrict the movement of goalkeepers with restraining lines. Adding more goals (or enlarging the ones you are using) is another way to increase goal production.

Goal production also increases when players improve their shooting technique (*how*) and tactical knowledge (*when* and *where*). As with passing skills, introduce shooting techniques as early as the beginner stage, but emphasize them more strongly in the later stages of development. One way to improve shooting skills is through drill work. Shooting drills develop the skills players need to score goals. Develop your players' shooting skills progressively. The drills in this chapter improve shooting skills using the following progression:

- Stationary ball shot by a stationary player
- Stationary ball shot by a moving player
- Moving ball shot by a stationary player
- Moving ball shot by a moving player
- Shooting opportunities with subtle, then gamelike, defensive pressure

Players need to learn how to strike the ball properly when shooting. They can often take shots from close range with the inside of the foot, much the same way they shoot a pass. Using the inside of the foot enhances shooting accuracy. Teach players to strike the ball using the instep of the foot (where the shoelaces are located) when more power is necessary; explain that this gives them more power than striking with the toes. To prevent striking the ball with the toes, players should point the toes downward toward the ground and lock the ankle of the kicking foot. Placement of the nonkicking foot affects the elevation of the shot. Players should learn to place the nonkicking foot slightly ahead of the ball to keep the shot low. To focus your players' attention on striking the ball, eliminate distractions such as moving balls, moving shooters, or defenders. Begin the drill progression with a stationary ball and a stationary shooter.

As shooting techniques improve, increase the challenge by putting the shooter in motion before she strikes the ball. Such motion will detract from the precision of striking initially, because the player's vision must serve a dual purpose. It must both help her negotiate space on her way to the ball and help her place her foot at the correct location on the ball.

As players gain confidence, increase the challenge by placing both shooter and ball in motion, creating a more gamelike situation. Make this transition easy for players by serving balls that are not bouncing, at a moderate speed. When their shooting competence improves, serve balls at various speeds and levels.

The final step in the progression of shooting drills requires developing tactical knowledge by adding defensive pressure. Begin with subtle pressure and then graduate them to more gamelike pressure. Keep these drills fast paced, and avoid having players stand in line by using many balls and all available goals. If necessary, create temporary goals. You may want to incorporate shooting drills as part of a circuit in which some team members practice shooting while others practice fast footwork, passing, and so forth.

Some of the drills in this chapter recommend that you encourage creative play by including wall passes, takeovers, and overlaps. Wall passes are two-player combinations in which one player passes to a teammate; the player who passed then moves in a different direction and receives the ball back from his teammate. A takeover is another example of a two-player combination; in this case the player with the ball moves in one direction while a teammate, moving in a different direction, goes by him and takes the ball. An overlap is a combination of movements that involve more than two players. For example, one player passes to a second player, while a third player runs ahead and outside of the first player. The player who received the pass from the first player then passes to the third player. The three-player combination shown in figure 6.4 on page 230 is an example of an overlap.

78   PARTNER STATIONARY SHOOTING DRILL

PURPOSE

To develop proper kicking techniques for shooting a stationary ball from a stationary position with no defensive pressure.

LEVEL

Beginner, advanced beginner

EQUIPMENT

1 soccer ball for every 2 players

TIME

10 minutes

PROCEDURE

1. Players scatter and partners stand 10 to 15 yards apart.
2. The partner without the ball assumes a goalkeeper's stance, with hands in a ready position (see figure).
3. The other partner approaches the stationary ball and shoots, trying to hit the partner.

KEY POINTS

Beginning players are sometimes inaccurate while shooting. It may be necessary to increase the number of goalkeepers a player is shooting toward so that players spend less time chasing errant balls. For example, space three goalkeepers in ready positions about 10 feet (1 m) apart, and have the shooter aim for the middle one. Reinforce the importance of accuracy over power during this drill. Encourage players to watch the foot strike the ball, and remind them to kick with the instep of the foot as opposed to the toes.

RELATED DRILLS

Drill 80: Run-and-Shoot Drill
Drill 84: Spin-Turn Shooting Drill

PARTNER STATIONARY SHOOTING DRILL

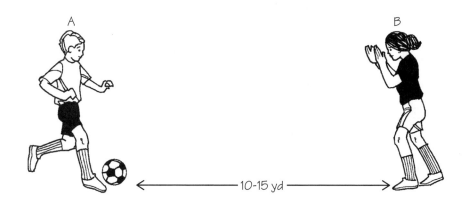

A

B

←——————— 10-15 yd ———————→

79 THREE-PLAYER SHOOTING DRILL

PURPOSE

To develop proper kicking technique for shooting a stationary ball from a stationary position, with no defensive pressure.

LEVEL

Advanced beginner, intermediate

EQUIPMENT

1 soccer ball for every 3 players

TIME

10 minutes

PROCEDURE

1. Three players stand in a line approximately 10 yards apart (see figure).
2. Player A shoots the ball at player B, who is in a goalkeeper's stance.
3. Player B collects the ball and rolls it to player C.
4. Player C stops the ball and then shoots at player B.
5. After several shots, players rotate.

KEY POINTS

Emphasize striking a stationary ball with the instep of the foot. Promote the philosophy of shooting accuracy over shooting power. As the players become more competent with shooting skills, increase the distance between them.

RELATED DRILLS

Drill 81: Reverse Serving Shooting Drill
Drill 82: Pass-and-Shoot Drill
Drill 83: Alternating Shooting Drill

80   RUN-AND-SHOOT DRILL

PURPOSE

To develop proper kicking technique when the shooter is in motion, the ball is stationary, and there is no defensive pressure.

LEVEL

Advanced beginner, intermediate

EQUIPMENT

- 4 soccer balls
- 1 goal
- 4 large game markers for every 4 players

TIME

10 minutes

PROCEDURE

Level 1

1. Place the four balls in a row in a 15- by 15-yard grid.
2. The shooter runs around one of the markers and shoots the ball into the goal.
3. The shooter repeats the action several times, running around a different marker each time, which creates variations for the angle of the kick.
4. During level 1, one player shoots, two players retrieve balls, and one resets the balls for the next shooter.

Level 2

1. Players repeat level 1, steps 1 and 2.
2. Place a goalkeeper outside each goalpost (see figure).
3. As the shooter makes the turn around the marker, signal one of the goalkeepers to step into one corner of the goal (just inside the goal on their side), which requires shooters to look up to determine where to place the ball.
4. The shooter must shoot to the unoccupied corner.
5. During level 2, one player shoots, two act as goalkeepers, and one retrieves balls.

KEY POINTS

You may want to use this drill as a station for circuit training. If you use this drill as a large-group activity, use both regular and temporary goals. Emphasize shooting low at the temporary goals and high at the regular goals.

RELATED DRILLS

Drill 78: Partner Stationary Shooting Drill
Drill 84: Spin-Turn Shooting Drill

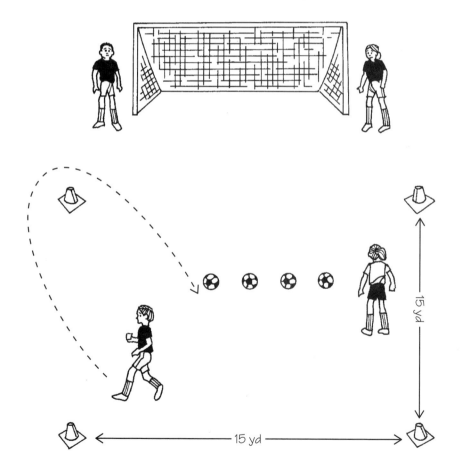

15 yd

15 yd

81 REVERSE SERVING SHOOTING DRILL

PURPOSE

To develop proper kicking technique for shooting a moving ball when the player is stationary and there is no defensive pressure.

LEVEL

Advanced beginner, intermediate, advanced

EQUIPMENT

6 soccer balls and 2 goals for every 5 players

TIME

15 minutes

PROCEDURE

1. Position two goals approximately 30 yards apart.
2. Place two players, D and B, on the sides with several balls.
3. Player C is the shooter (see figure).
4. When player B serves the ball, player C shoots at goalkeeper A.
5. When player D serves the ball, player C reverses and shoots at goalkeeper E.
6. After six shots, everyone rotates.

KEY POINTS

This drill is more gamelike than the preceding drills and highlights the role of target players. Putting the ball in motion reduces the shooter's time for making decisions. Point out that shooters must visually track the path of the foot as it strikes the ball and must also adjust for the speed, direction, and level of the ball. To make this process less complicated for less skilled players, have servers serve balls at a moderate speed and a flat level. As skills improve, players may practice shooting balls served at various speeds and levels.

RELATED DRILLS

Drill 79: Three-Player Shooting Drill
Drill 82: Pass-and-Shoot Drill
Drill 83: Alternating Shooting Drill

82 PASS-AND-SHOOT DRILL

PURPOSE

To develop proper kicking technique for shooting a moving ball when the player is stationary and there is no defensive pressure.

LEVEL

Advanced beginner, intermediate, advanced

EQUIPMENT

1 or more soccer balls and 2 goals for every 4 players

TIME

15 minutes

PROCEDURE

1. Place two goals 30 yards apart.
2. Position players as shown (see figure).
3. Player B serves to player C, who shoots at goalkeeper D.
4. Goalkeeper D passes to player C. Player C passes to player B, who shoots at goalkeeper A.
5. Players repeat the action several times and then change roles.

KEY POINTS

Keep several balls in the goals for goalkeepers to pass so the drill stays fast paced. Encourage one-touch shooting to the corners of the goals.

RELATED DRILLS

Drill 79: Three-Player Shooting Drill
Drill 81: Reverse Serving Shooting Drill
Drill 83: Alternating Shooting Drill

83 ALTERNATING SHOOTING DRILL

PURPOSE

To develop proper kicking technique for shooting a moving ball when the player is moving and there is no defensive pressure.

LEVEL

Intermediate, advanced

EQUIPMENT

4 soccer balls and 1 set of goals for every 4 players

TIME

10 minutes

PROCEDURE

1. Place two goals 30 yards apart.
2. Position two players in the center of the field (see figure).
3. Player B serves balls alternately right and left to player A.
4. Player A must go after the ball and shoot at the goal toward which the ball is traveling.
5. Player A then returns to shoot in the opposite direction.

KEY POINTS

Moving players who are shooting moving balls must gather a lot of information in a short time. They must compute the direction, speed, and level of the ball; their own speed; their angle to the ball; their level relative to the ball; the distance from goal; and the position of the goalkeeper. This is why combining a moving ball and a moving player is the final step in the shooting progression.

RELATED DRILLS

Drill 79: Three-Player Shooting Drill
Drill 81: Reverse Serving Shooting Drill
Drill 82: Pass-and-Shoot Drill

84 SPIN-TURN SHOOTING DRILL

PURPOSE

To develop the ability to create space for shooting a moving ball when the player is moving and there is no defensive pressure.

LEVEL

Intermediate, advanced

EQUIPMENT

1 soccer ball and 1 goal for every 2 players

TIME

10 minutes

PROCEDURE

1. Position players in the offensive third of the field.
2. Player A, in the penalty box, makes a horizontal run and then checks back for the ball (see figure).
3. Player B passes to player A, who returns the ball to player B with a one-touch pass.
4. After returning the pass, player A spins to the outside to create space for player B to return the pass for a shot at goal.

KEY POINTS

Players should pivot on the inside foot (the foot closer to the goal) when spinning to the outside. Players should alternate between spinning wide to create enough space for a pass, and spinning close to the defender to get behind her.

RELATED DRILLS

Drill 78: Partner Stationary Shooting Drill
Drill 80: Run-and-Shoot Drill

85   BOMBARDMENT GAME

PURPOSE

To develop shooting skills with subtle defensive pressure.

LEVEL

Intermediate, advanced

EQUIPMENT

- 1 soccer ball for each player
- 4 large game markers
- 1 portable goal

TIME

10 minutes

PROCEDURE

1. Position players as shown in the figure.
2. On your signal, player A1 shoots the ball at the goal, trying to score against player B1.
3. If player A1 is successful, player A2 shoots the ball, trying to score against a new goalkeeper (player B2).
4. If player A1 is unsuccessful, she becomes the goalkeeper and moves to the side of the goal where player B1 shoots at the goal to try to score.
5. If player B1 scores, player B2 shoots at the goal, where player A2 is now the goalkeeper. Player A1, who was replaced by player A2, will go to the end of the line.
6. The action continues until one team scores 10 goals and is declared the winner.

KEY POINTS

This game provides lots of scoring opportunities. Encourage players to use a variety of shooting techniques including using the inside of the foot, the outside of the foot, and the instep. As players begin to score more easily, challenge them by reducing the size of the goal or increasing the distance from which they must shoot.

RELATED DRILLS

Drill 86: 3v1 Shooting Drill
Drill 88: Come-and-Get-Me Shooting Drill

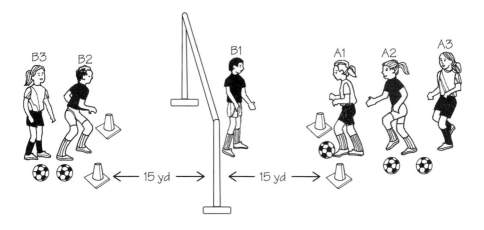

86   3v1 SHOOTING DRILL

PURPOSE

To develop proper kicking techniques for shooting a moving ball when the player is moving and there is subtle defensive pressure.

LEVEL

Intermediate, advanced

EQUIPMENT

- 1 soccer ball and 1 goal for every 4 players
- 1 jersey for every goalkeeper

TIME

10 minutes

PROCEDURE

Level 1

1. Position players approximately 30 yards from the goal (see figure).
2. Offensive players A, B, and C connect a series of passes until one of them takes a shot for the goal.
3. One defender provides subtle pressure.

Level 2

1. Players repeat level 1, steps 1 and 2.
2. A goalkeeper provides more defensive pressure.

KEY POINTS

Every offensive player must have touched the ball before any one of them can take a shot. Encourage creative movements such as switching and overlapping runs. Giving offensive players a numbers advantage such as this drill gives them more opportunities to score goals.

3v1 SHOOTING DRILL

RELATED DRILLS

Drill 85: Bombardment Game
Drill 88: Come-and-Get-Me Shooting Drill

87 CAT-AND-MOUSE SHOOTING DRILL

PURPOSE

To develop the ability to create space for shooting with subtle defensive pressure.

LEVEL

Intermediate, advanced

EQUIPMENT

1 soccer ball and 1 goal for every 2 players

TIME

10 minutes

PROCEDURE

1. Position players as shown in the figure.
2. Player A passes to player B.
3. Player A then makes a bending run to offer passive defense against player B's penetrating moves.
4. Player B collects the ball and completes one or more moves to create space for a shot.

KEY POINTS

Player A must wait for player B to collect the ball before making his bending run. Emphasize subtle pressure by the defender because this is an offensive drill. Encourage a variety of moves by offensive players. To allow more scoring, do not use a goalkeeper initially. Use as many goals as possible.

RELATED DRILLS

None

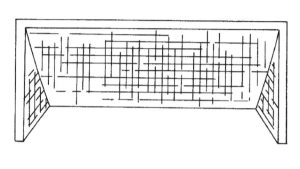

88   COME-AND-GET-ME
SHOOTING DRILL

PURPOSE

To develop the ability to create space for shooting with subtle defensive pressure.

LEVEL

Intermediate, advanced

EQUIPMENT

1 soccer ball and 1 goal for every 3 players

TIME

10 minutes

PROCEDURE

1. Position players in the offensive third of the field.
2. Player A runs away from the ball, then checks back toward it and receives a pass from player B (see figure).
3. When player B touches the ball, player C runs to defend against player A.
4. Player A must create space to shoot using individual moves.
5. Player C is passive in playing defense.

KEY POINTS

Initially, space the server and the defender far enough apart so the offensive player has a distinct advantage. As players' skills improve, move the defender closer to reduce the time the attacker has to shoot.

RELATED DRILLS

Drill 85: Bombardment Game
Drill 86: 3v1 Shooting Drill

COME-AND-GET-ME
SHOOTING DRILL

89 DOUBLE-DEFENDED SHOOTING DRILL

PURPOSE

To develop the ability to create space for shooting with gamelike defensive pressure.

LEVEL

Advanced

EQUIPMENT

- 6 soccer balls
- 5 large game markers
- 1 goal

TIME

15 minutes

PROCEDURE

1. Position players as shown in the figure.
2. On your signal, player A passes the ball to player B. Player A then runs to defend player B to prevent him from shooting.
3. When player B touches the ball passed from player A, player C sprints after him and defends. Player A is now double defended.
4. Player B tries to score while being defended by two players.
5. After the play, player A moves to game marker 3, player B moves to game marker 1, and player C moves to game marker 2.
6. Players repeat the action.

KEY POINTS

This drill replicates game conditions in which defenders are challenging in front of and behind the player in possession of the ball. Encourage players to quickly assess the defenders' positions and create space for shooting opportunities. Begin this drill without a goalkeeper to allow for lots of opportunities to score. As players progress, increase the difficulty and make the drill more gamelike by adding a goalkeeper.

DOUBLE-DEFENDED SHOOTING DRILL

RELATED DRILLS

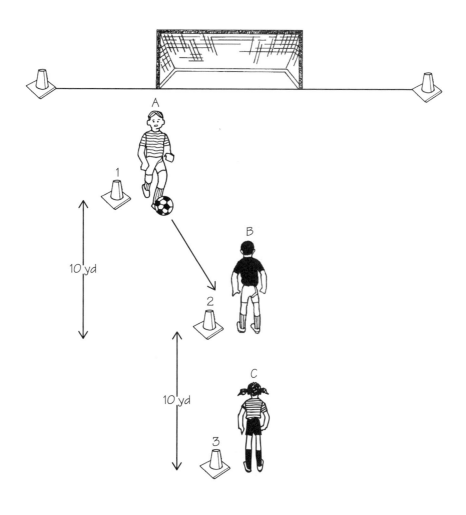

90

TEAM CHALLENGE
SHOOTING GAME

PURPOSE

To develop the ability to create space for shooting opportunities under gamelike defensive pressure.

LEVEL

Advanced beginner, intermediate, advanced

EQUIPMENT

- 6 soccer balls
- 2 goals
- 4 large game markers

TIME

15 minutes

PROCEDURE

Level 1

1. Position two teams of three players on opposite sides of a 20-by 30-yard grid as shown in the figure.
2. On your signal, the first player from each team enters the grid.
3. Serve a ball to the two players in the grid.
4. The player who gains possession of the ball tries to score at her designated goal.
5. Whichever team scores 5 goals first is the winner.

Level 2

Have players repeat the procedure for level 1, but with goalkeepers.

KEY POINTS

This is a fast-paced drill that provides lots of shooting opportunities. Have players shoot initially without goalkeepers to increase their confidence. Add goalkeepers at level 2 and encourage players to use good visual techniques to locate the goalkeeper before shooting. Encourage those who shoot to retrieve the ball and quickly return it to you. This will keep the game fast paced. Challenge players by adding variations such as restricting the number of touches or mandating that they use the left foot only, the right foot only, the outside of foot, or the instep.

RELATED DRILLS

Drill 89: Double-Defended Shooting Drill
Drill 92: Add-On Shooting Game
Drill 93: Wall Pass Shooting Drill
Drill 98: Sideline Shooting Game
Drill 99: Double-Sided Shooting Game

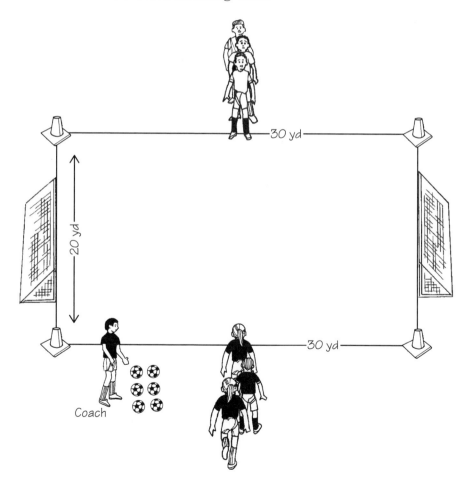

91   YOU-AND-ME SHOOTING GAME

PURPOSE

To develop the ability to create space for shooting opportunities under gamelike defensive pressure.

LEVEL

Advanced beginner, intermediate, advanced

EQUIPMENT

- 6 soccer balls
- 2 goals
- 4 large game markers

TIME

2 minutes

PROCEDURE

Level 1

1. Position two players in a 20- by 20-yard grid with two goals at opposite ends as shown in the figure.
2. On your signal, player A tries to create space to shoot at her designated goal while being defended. If player B steals the ball, he tries to shoot at his own goal.
3. If player A scores, player B retrieves a ball from the goal he is defending and tries to create space to shoot at his designated goal while being defended.
4. The game continues for two minutes. The player who scores the most goals wins the game.

Level 2

Have players repeat the procedure for level 1, but with goalkeepers.

YOU-AND-ME SHOOTING GAME 91

KEY POINTS

This is a very simple drill with lots of action. Encourage players to shoot from varying distances and angles and to focus while fatigued. During level 2 action, emphasize the correct placement of shots according to the goalkeeper's positioning. Wait until after the drill to make corrections. If possible, have several pairs of players play this game at the same time or while the rest of the team is involved in a small-sided game or other activity.

RELATED DRILLS

None

92   ADD-ON SHOOTING GAME

PURPOSE

To develop shooting techniques and tactics under various degrees of defensive pressure.

LEVEL

Intermediate, advanced

EQUIPMENT

- 6 soccer balls
- 2 goals
- 3 blue scrimmage jerseys and 3 red scrimmage jerseys
- 4 large game markers

TIME

15 minutes

PROCEDURE

Level 1

1. Position one player from the blue team and one player from the red team in a 20- by 20-yard grid. Two players for each team stand on opposite sidelines (see figure). Place goals at opposite ends with no goalkeepers.

2. Begin play by dropping the ball between the players in the grid.

3. The player controlling the ball tries to score at her designated goal while being defended. If the defender steals the ball, she then tries to score at her designated goal.

4. The team that scores first adds another player. The game begins again by your dropping the ball. This time, however, the team that scored has a 2v1 advantage.

5. If the team that scored first scores again, another player is added, giving that team a 3v1 advantage. However, if the opponent scores next, play continues 2v2. At no time will any team have more than three players competing.

6. Play continues until one of the teams scores 5 goals and is declared the winner.

Level 2

Have players repeat the procedure for level 1, but with goalkeepers.

KEY POINTS

This drill offers endless opportunities for developing shooting techniques and tactics. It rewards teams for scoring by allowing them to add an extra player. Emphasize the role of the second attacker (the teammate closest to the player with the ball, who provides support to her) and that of the third attacker (the player who provides opportunities to gain space behind the defenders).

RELATED DRILLS

Drill 89: Double-Defended Shooting Drill
Drill 90: Team Challenge Shooting Game
Drill 93: Wall Pass Shooting Drill
Drill 98: Sideline Shooting Game
Drill 99: Double-Sided Shooting Game

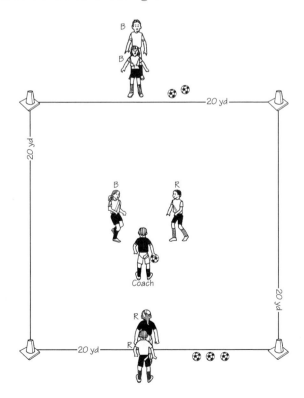

93 WALL PASS SHOOTING DRILL

PURPOSE

To develop the ability to create space for shooting with gamelike defensive pressure.

LEVEL

Intermediate, advanced

EQUIPMENT

1 soccer ball and 1 goal for every 4 players

TIME

10 minutes

PROCEDURE

Level 1

1. Position players in the defensive third of the field (see figure).
2. Player A is the offensive player; player B is the defender.
3. Player A passes to player C or player D as targets, then moves to open space for a return pass and shot.
4. Player B defends aggressively.

Level 2

1. The ball is served to player A.
2. Player A must collect the ball and take on the defender with individual moves to create space for a shot, or use players C and D for wall passes.

Level 3

1. Players repeat level 2, steps 1 and 2.
2. A goalkeeper increases defensive pressure.

KEY POINTS

Encourage players to change speed and use quick bursts to create spaces for shots.

WALL PASS SHOOTING DRILL 93

RELATED DRILLS

Drill 89: Double-Defended Shooting Drill
Drill 90: Team Challenge Shooting Game
Drill 92: Add-On Shooting Game
Drill 98: Sideline Shooting Game
Drill 99: Double-Sided Shooting Game

94   1v1 FOR ALL DRILL

PURPOSE

To develop dribbling skills and learn to create space for shooting opportunities with gamelike defensive pressure.

LEVEL

Advanced beginner, intermediate, advanced

EQUIPMENT

1 soccer ball and 2 goals for every 8 players

TIME

10 minutes

PROCEDURE

1. Arrange eight players with goals approximately 30 yards apart, as shown in the figure.
2. Player A dribbles toward goal 1 in an attempt to score.
3. Player B defends.
4. After player A shoots, he becomes the defender, and player B moves approximately 10 yards to the outside of the goal he defended.
5. Player C, who is waiting on the side of the goal that player B defended, becomes the new offensive player.
6. Player C receives a pass from the goalie and dribbles toward goal 2, which is approximately 30 yards away, while player A defends.
7. After player C shoots, he becomes the defender, and so on.
8. A defender who steals the ball becomes the offensive player.
9. The defending player always goes to the side of the goal he defended.
10. Players rotate from offensive player, to defensive player, to standing at the side of the goal.

KEY POINTS

This drill is very intensive. Limiting the number of players to eight maximizes the number of touches, yet allows for brief recovery periods. Present this drill initially with no goalkeepers to make scoring easier. As players' skills improve, add a goalkeeper to increase the defensive pressure.

RELATED DRILLS

Drill 95: Never-Ending 3v2 Drill
Drill 96: Shooting Combination Drill

95 NEVER-ENDING 3v2 DRILL

PURPOSE

To develop combination play to create shooting opportunities with gamelike defensive pressure.

LEVEL

Intermediate, advanced

EQUIPMENT

1 soccer ball and 2 goals for every 7 players

TIME

10 minutes

PROCEDURE

1. Place two goals approximately 30 yards apart.
2. Position three offensive players in the middle of the field, ready to score against two defenders (see figure).
3. Position two defenders at each end of the field.
4. On your signal, the three offensive players pass the ball among themselves until they get close enough to the goal to shoot.
5. The player who takes the shot then joins the two defenders from this goal to try to score against the two defenders at the opposite end of the field. The other two offensive players become defenders at the goal they shot at.
6. If a defender steals a pass, that defending pair goes on the attack with the person from whom they stole the pass. The other offensive players become defenders at the goal at which they were trying to score.

KEY POINTS

The offensive players have a numbers advantage, so there should always be an open player. Encourage players to make switching and overlapping runs to create space. Challenge them by allowing them no more than two touches on the ball.

RELATED DRILLS

Drill 94: 1v1 for All Drill

Drill 96: Shooting Combination Drill

96 SHOOTING COMBINATION DRILL

PURPOSE

To develop shooting techniques and tactics under various degrees of defensive pressure.

LEVEL

Advanced

EQUIPMENT

- 4 soccer balls
- 1 goal
- 6 large game markers
- 12 jerseys (6 red, 6 blue)

TIME

20 minutes

PROCEDURE

1. Position four game markers in a straight line 10 yards apart and 30 yards from the goal. Place two additional markers to the side of each goalpost (see figure).

2. Two players, one red and one blue, stand at each of the six markers. A goalkeeper is in the goal.

3. The drill begins with the red team on offense and the blue team on defense.

4. On your signal, the red player from game marker 1 speed dribbles to the goal and shoots. The blue defender must start in a sitting position.

5. On your second signal, the red player at game marker 2 passes to the red player from game marker 5, who has just made a diagonal run. The blue player at game marker 2 does not defend against this pass. The red player from game marker 2 then moves to support the red player from game marker 5 in an attempt to have either player shoot. Blue players from game markers 2 and 5 defend.

6. The same action is repeated at your third signal by players at game markers 3 and 6.

7. On your fourth signal, the red player from game marker 4 must take on the blue defender from game marker 4 one on one. The red player from game marker 4 attempts to drive toward the goal and shoot.

8. Players return to their markers after they finish their tasks. When all players are finished, they rotate to the next marker (1 to 2, 2 to 3, and so forth; 6 rotates to 1).

9. When all players have completed the cycle, the teams switch offensive and defensive roles.

KEY POINTS

Players need to practice shooting from various angles and under varying circumstances. Encourage players to use good visual techniques to locate the position of the goalkeeper. Remind them that placement of the shot is more important than its power.

RELATED DRILLS

Drill 94: 1v1 for All Drill
Drill 95: Never-Ending 3v2 Drill

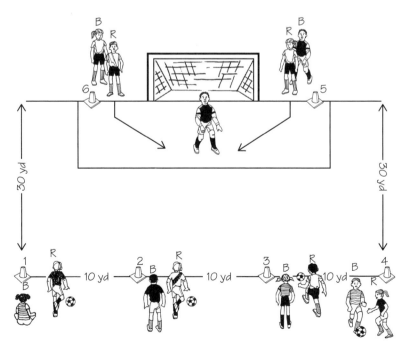

97   TARGET DRILL

PURPOSE

To develop combination play in the offensive third of the field.

LEVEL

Advanced

EQUIPMENT

- 1 soccer ball
- 2 large game markers
- 1 goal

TIME

20 minutes

PROCEDURE

1. Position two game markers 10 yards apart and 30 yards from the goal (see figure).
2. Players A and B take positions behind an imaginary line between the markers. Players C and D (target players) are stationed between the goal and the markers. A goalkeeper is positioned in the goal.
3. On your signal, players A and B pass the ball back and forth as players C and D make various types of runs (lateral, switching, and diagonal) to open space.
4. Player A or B passes to player C or D.
5. Players C and D must execute a combination play (e.g., takeover, overlap, wall pass) before shooting.
6. Players repeat the action several times and then change roles.

KEY POINTS

This drill is the first stage in developing combination play for use in the attacking third of the field. Encourage players to use vision, communication, and movement to develop creative play. Once they demonstrate an understanding of combination plays, make the drill more gamelike by adding one or two defenders. When using one defender, the first pass from player A or B must go to the target player being defended against. This drill can also be modified to develop the role of the third attacker by allowing either player A or player B to go forward, creating a 3v2 situation. The player going forward should be the one who did not pass the ball forward (e.g., player A passes and player B makes a run forward).

RELATED DRILL

Drill 100: Framing Drill

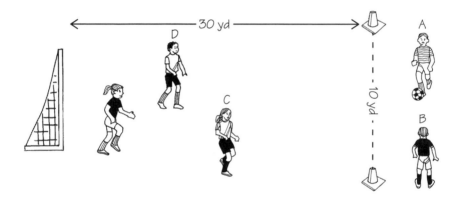

98   SIDELINE SHOOTING GAME

PURPOSE

To develop combination play and shooting skills under gamelike defensive pressure.

LEVEL

Intermediate, advanced

EQUIPMENT

- 1 soccer ball
- 4 red scrimmage jerseys and 4 blue scrimmage jerseys
- 2 goals
- 4 large game markers

TIME

20 minutes

PROCEDURE

1. Position players as shown in the figure.
2. Play begins by your designating which goalkeeper plays the ball to a teammate.
3. Players inside the grid play 2v2, trying to score at their designated goals.
4. Players inside the grid may pass to the sideline players to create 3v2 situations. Sideline players may not enter the grid and may not be defended.
5. After five minutes of action, the sideline players switch with the players inside the grid and play continues.
6. The team with the most goals after 20 minutes is declared the winner.

KEY POINTS

This fast-paced drill provides numerous opportunities for goal scoring and combination play. Emphasize the role of the second attacker (the teammate closest to the player with the ball, who provides support). Encourage creative play that includes wall passes, takeovers, and overlaps. You may choose to use the Sideline Shooting Game to teach how to defend shooting and two-player combination plays. If you do, emphasize the role of the second defender (the player who defends against the opponent's second attacker and who is responsible for supplying cover to the first defender).

RELATED DRILLS

Drill 89: Double-Defended Shooting Drill
Drill 90: Team Challenge Shooting Game
Drill 92: Add-On Shooting Game
Drill 93: Wall Pass Shooting Drill
Drill 99: Double-Sided Shooting Game

99 DOUBLE-SIDED SHOOTING GAME

PURPOSE

To develop shooting accuracy and combination play with gamelike defensive pressure.

LEVEL

Advanced

EQUIPMENT

- 6 soccer balls
- 3 red scrimmage jerseys and 3 blue scrimmage jerseys
- 6 large game markers

TIME

20 minutes

PROCEDURE

1. Position players in a 20- by 20-yard grid as shown in the figure.
2. Position two game markers in the middle of the grid with a goalkeeper between the markers as shown in the figure.
3. To begin play, serve the ball to the side of the grid where there are two sets of players.
4. If, for example, player A1 gains possession of the ball, he may shoot, play the ball to player A2, or play it to the opposite side of the grid to player A3. If player A1 plays the ball to player A3, he may go to that side of the grid. His defender follows.
5. If the ball is taken from team A, team B tries to score but must first play it to the opposite side of the grid. Teams may score from either side of the grid.
6. If a goal is scored or a ball is played outside of the grid, put another ball in play.
7. If the goalkeeper saves a shot, she may play it to either side of the grid to a member of the nonshooting team.
8. At least one member of each team must be on each side of the grid at all times.
9. At the conclusion of 20 minutes, the team with the most goals is declared the winner.

KEY POINTS

Encourage the use of combination play such as takeovers, wall passes, and overlaps to create shooting opportunities. Challenge players to be creative as they use vision, communication, and movement to create spaces for passing and shooting opportunities. Using a portable goal without a net (or two game markers spaced 8 yards apart) will give the goalkeeper a better chance to defend both sides of the grid. Explain to players that, to score a goal, they must pass the ball between the markers in the middle of the grid and below the goalkeeper's shoulders.

RELATED DRILLS

Drill 89: Double-Defended Shooting Drill
Drill 90: Team Challenge Shooting Game
Drill 92: Add-On Shooting Game
Drill 93: Wall Pass Shooting Drill
Drill 98: Sideline Shooting Game

100   FRAMING DRILL

PURPOSE

To develop the ability to take shots from crossing balls.

LEVEL

Advanced

EQUIPMENT

- 4 balls
- 2 goals

TIME

20 minutes

PROCEDURE

1. Position players as shown in the figure.
2. On your signal, player A passes to player B, who checks to the ball.
3. Player B passes back to player A, then pivots to the outside and runs down the sideline to receive a return pass (long ball) from player A. Player A then assumes the position at midfield that was just vacated by player B.
4. Player B dribbles the ball to the corner and crosses the ball.
5. Player 1, 2, or 3 attempts a shot off the crossing ball and then regroups for the next cross.
6. At the time player A starts the action on the right side of the field, player C starts the same action on the left side, passing to player D.
7. As soon as player A repositions herself at midfield, player E passes a ball to her.
8. After crossing the ball, player B runs to the corner where player C started, on the opposite side of the field, behind player F. Player C continues the action after player F has taken his turn. Player D, after crossing, runs to the corner where players A and E started the action.
9. After several crosses, players switch roles.

KEY POINTS

When they are positioning for crossing balls, encourage player 1 to make a near-post run, player 2 to position herself near the penalty kick line, and player 3 to make a far-post run. Instruct players serving the crossing balls to serve flat passes for near-post runs, waist-high balls for the penalty kick mark, and lofted balls for far-post runs. Insist that players 1, 2, and 3 regroup quickly outside the box as soon as one crossing ball is played so they can time their runs at proper angles for the next cross. Promote creativity by allowing players in the box to make switching runs. To create a more gamelike atmosphere, add one defender in the box at first, and then a second and third defender.

RELATED DRILL

Drill 97: Target Drill

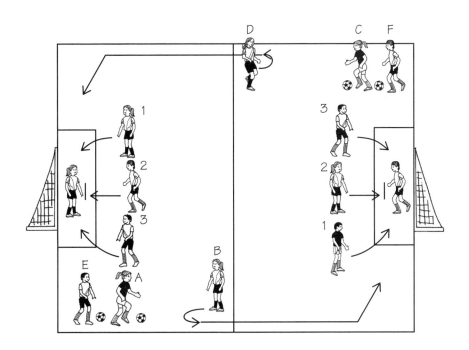

6

Game Progressions

he progression of player development in games begins with a focus on skill acquisition and movement concepts. Limit the number of players in a game at first so they have more time and space for making decisions. This ensures that players get plenty of touches on the ball and makes them more accountable for their choices (because there are fewer people to do the job). As players become more skilled and their knowledge base increases, the player development process progresses with the addition of more players, more rules, larger fields, and more team strategies. The process suffers when coaches emphasize competition too early, confuse players with soccer terminology prematurely, or implement burdensome rules and structure on beginners.

It would be impossible to discuss all of the changes in strategies, concepts, and so forth that occur at each level of learning. Instead, I will discuss some of the major concerns and recommend this series of game setups: 4v4, 5v5, 8v8, and 11v11. This sequence is not an original idea of mine. The Dutch developed this teaching model, which I have used as a guideline but have modified somewhat. This progression varies somewhat from the one I used in my early coaching experience. I have adopted this model because it provides an easy transition from one level to the next for both players and coaches.

4v4

The 4v4, small-sided game works well for beginning players ages 5 and 6. It should be played on a field approximately 50 yards long by 30 yards wide. Goal size should be developmentally appropriate for the age and size of the players. I recommend a goal about 8 feet (2.4 m) wide and 5 feet (1.5 m) high. The rules of the modified 4v4 game are intentionally very simple so players can concentrate on the new skills and movement concepts they are learning without the burden of numerous rules.

Start the game with a kickoff, and use a kickoff after either team scores a goal. If a team kicks the ball out of bounds over the touchline, the opposite team receives a throw-in opportunity. If either team kicks the ball over the end line, the team whose goal is on that line gets a free kick. The nonkicking team must retreat to the half-field line, wait for the opposing team to take the kick, and then pursue the ball.

The 4v4 game changes the traditional rules for corner kicks and goal kicks. There are no goalkeepers. This adaptation is somewhat controversial among soccer coaches, but it allows teams to score many goals, reduces collisions, and diminishes injuries.

In front of the goal is a safety zone, similar to a goal box, which no one may enter unless the ball is there. If the ball is there, either team may enter. This rule allows the offense to finish a play and the defense to stop a scoring opportunity, but it prohibits the defense from camping in front of the goal. The game includes no offside rules or penalty kicks, and all penalties result in a free kick from the spot of the foul. To get the best results with this game, have eight players on the field (four from each team) and eight players on the sidelines. The eight on the field play for five to seven minutes. Then the eight who were on the sidelines switch places with the field players. Children this age need a break after five to seven minutes of continuous motion. The 4v4 model allows for continuous motion with hundreds of opportunities for collection and distribution. It also allows for numerous goal-scoring opportunities. The game should last approximately 30 minutes.

5v5

The 5v5 game works well for players 7 and 8 years of age. It is the same game as 4v4—played on a 50- by 30-yard field, but with the addition of corner kicks and a goalkeeper. The goalkeeper may not come outside the safety zone, and no player is allowed inside the safety zone (even if the ball is inside the zone).

The goalkeeper adds new dimensions to the game. The attack must not only penetrate the defense but also beat the goalkeeper. The defense must reckon with the transition game after the goalkeeper collects the ball and initiates the attack. Give everyone who wants to experience the goalkeeper position a chance to do so. Some children, however, will not want the opportunity because of the fear factor. Do not insist that these children play in the goal.

Teach only basic goalkeeping skills at this level. You should instruct goalkeepers to get their bodies behind their hands whenever possible and to position their hands correctly (thumbs in for balls above the waist, thumbs out for balls below the waist). They should catch and hold whenever possible, and position themselves at the proper angle to reduce the space from which an attacker can shoot. Continue to refer to the team shape (diamond) and positions of players (flank, forward, defender) during instruction.

Collecting, Looking, and Decision Making

The 5v5 game offers hundreds of opportunities to touch the ball. With only five players from each team on the field, players have the time and space to practice the process of collecting, looking, and decision making. Encourage them to use this process. Initially, players tend to engage in a kick-and-run style. With patient teaching of the distribution process, you will find that players demonstrate better use of space when in possession of the ball and that the game begins to have more structure. As players develop skills and the pace of the game quickens, the process changes to looking, collecting, and decision making. Players at this level, however, are not yet ready for this advanced progression. At this level, allow some time in the game for the players to play without guidance.

Support and Balance

Players at this level should be familiar with moving to support positions away from the person with the ball (open space) instead of moving to the space of the person who has the ball (closed space). The player who collects the ball must then look and make a decision about where to play the ball next. You should emphasize proper spacing of supporting players to help eliminate a swarming effect around the ball. The five-player team model aids proper spacing. This model includes a goalkeeper and aligns four other field players in the shape of a diamond so they may play the ball in any direction—forward, backward, or sideways (left or right).

As figure 6.1 shows, player A provides length, players B and C provide width, player D provides depth, and player E is the goalkeeper. After the player passes the ball, he moves to a new support position. Continue to reinforce the concept of moving, both with and without the ball, while maintaining a good team shape.

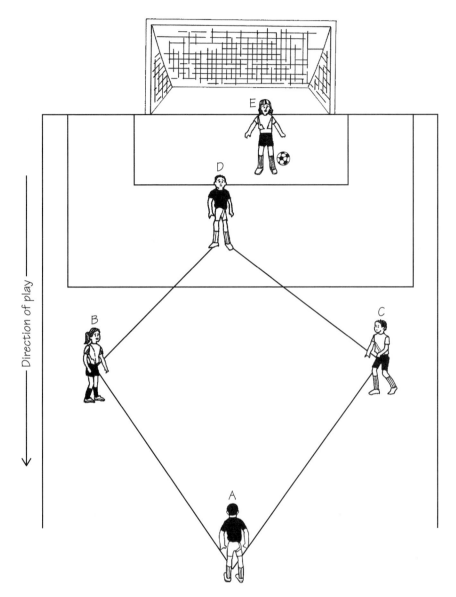

Figure 6.1 Single-diamond team shape (five-player team model).

Maintaining the team shape (a diamond) helps ensure good field balance (spacing). I also recommend that you give your players the opportunity to play each of the four field positions in the diamond formation. Identify these positions and constantly refer to them by name during practice: forward, defender, right flank, left flank.

225

Explain the roles of these positions simply. The forward stays near midfield when the other team has the ball (to provide length), and closer to her goal when her team has the ball. The flank players pinch toward the middle of the field and stay goalside of their opponent when playing defense, but move outside toward the touchlines (to provide width) when on offense. The defender stays back near her goal when on defense (to provide depth) and moves forward when on offense (to provide support), but must remember to keep the team shape.

Remind players that defending is not the sole responsibility of the goalkeeper and the player in the back of the diamond, and that if everyone pushes forward on attack (swarming around the ball), the defense will lack depth. Using drills that require spacing of players (e.g., Monkey-in-the-Middle Drill), teaching the roles of players in an uncomplicated fashion and constantly referring to the names of these positions (forward, flank, defender) should reduce the swarming effect so prevalent in this age group. Be patient. It takes time for players to fully understand and demonstrate the notions of support and balance; however, these are critical building blocks for the next level.

8v8

Use the 8v8 game for players 9 and 10 years old. Play this game on a field approximately 70 yards long and 40 yards wide. Goals should be approximately 6 feet (1.8 m) high and 12 feet (3.7 m) wide. Each team has seven field players and one goalkeeper. Explain the role of each player during kickoffs, throw-ins, goal kicks, corner kicks, free kicks, and penalty kicks, because regulation rules apply at this level.

The addition of three more players than at the previous level challenges the players' ability, because they will have less time and space for technical execution and tactical decisions. The three players are added to the basic diamond shape—one as a forward, one as a defender, and one as a central midfielder—so that the team shape now has the appearance of two diamonds (see figure 6.2).

Players at this level should understand basic skills and techniques and concepts of space and movement. Play is more struc-

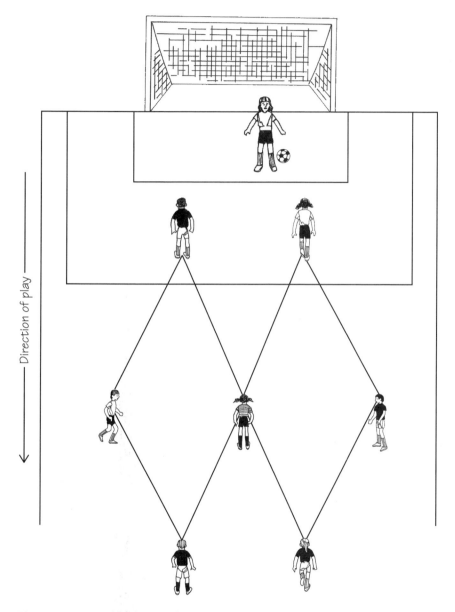

Figure 6.2 Double-diamond team shape (eight-player team model).

tured, and you can expect more advanced results. Explain and discuss new concepts, such as the roles of various players:

- First attacker—the player with the ball, whose role is to pene-trate the defense

- Second attacker—the teammate who is closest to the player with the ball and who provides support to him
- Third attacker—all other players who provide opportunities to gain space behind the defenders
- First defender—the player who pressures the opponent in possession of the ball
- Second defender—the player who defends against the opponent's second attacker and who is also responsible for supplying cover for the first defender
- Third defender—all other defenders who provide proper spacing and field balance
- Central midfielder—the player who provides a link for the transition from defense to offense and who provides depth to relieve pressure on the forwards
- Goalkeeper—the player who defends against a variety of crossing balls and who helps relieve pressure on defenders during transitions

Discuss how the role of the goalkeeper has expanded in 8v8 because she is no longer confined to a safety zone (as in 5v5). Other topics to address include the relationship between the two forwards (combination play and spacing) and the relationship between the two defenders (spacing and support, to deny penetration and provide cover).

Team tactics are more complex at this level. Introduce more sophisticated attacking and defending tactics and set plays. Also, emphasize the importance of using field width and diagonal movement in attacking tactics. Using the width of the field stretches the defense, which creates passing lanes. The defenders must choose between defending the width, which allows passing lanes on the inside, and compacting the defense, which allows passes to the outside. Diagonal movement, instead of only forward and backward movement, creates better visual space for players. Creating better visual space opens up the field so that players may choose from several possibilities for penetrating the defense.

Introduce this age group to defensive team tactics. Tactical choices include which defensive scheme to use (zone, man to man, or a zone/man combination) and how to defend in various areas of the field (offensive third, middle third, and defensive third). As a rule, the closer the ball is to a team's goal, the more compact the defensive unit should be.

Using Space Creatively

Players at this level are ready to explore the use of creative movements without the ball, including diagonal runs, lateral runs, overlaps, switches, and takeovers. Diagonal runs allow players to receive the ball with better vision (because they can see more of the field). They are effective at this level because players now have the ability to make longer passes. Such movements give the defense something different to look at and thus cause confusion. Players generally make vertical or diagonal runs to create space for themselves, and horizontal runs to create space for teammates.

You should incorporate into each practice session drills that emphasize using space creatively. These drills should include two-player combinations and plays involving more than two players.

A two-player combination can be simple, as when a player dribbles in one direction and a teammate comes from the opposite direction, takes the ball from him, and continues dribbling (a takeover). Another example of a two-player combination is a switch. Figure 6.3 shows a simple switch that you can use as a finishing drill. After player A collects the ball in the corner, he can cross the ball to player B, who is

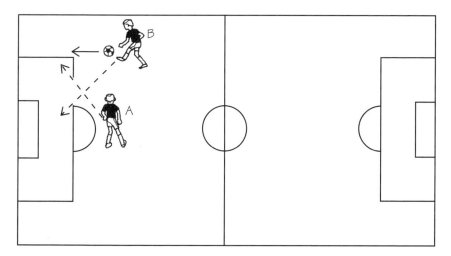

Figure 6.3 Simple switch.

making a run to goal for a shot. There are also combinations of movement using more than two players. Figure 6.4 shows player B passing to player A, and then player C running ahead and outside of player B to receive a pass from player A. This sequence is a three-player combination using an overlapping run by player C. Figure 6.5 shows a four-player combination. After player C collects the ball, she crosses to player D, who is making a diagonal run to the goal.

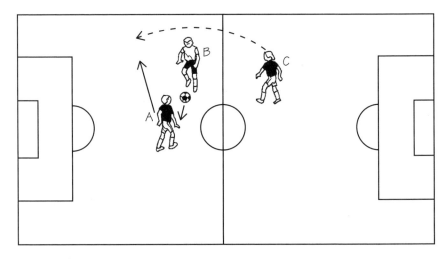

Figure 6.4   Three-player combination.

Figure 6.5   Four-player combination.

Set Plays

Set plays contribute to greater structure in the game and should be introduced at this level. When creating these plays, strive for simplicity. Complicated patterns of movement only frustrate players at this stage. Evaluate the players' abilities and design plays they can execute. Many game situations call for set plays, including kickoffs, corner kicks, goal kicks, direct free kicks, indirect free kicks, penalty kicks, and throw-ins.

11v11

By the time the players are 11 years old, they should be ready to play on a larger field, approximately 100 yards long and 60 yards wide. The goals should be regulation size—8 feet (2.4 m) high by 24 feet (7.3 m) wide. The official rules of soccer apply at this level.

You should continue to review and refine skills and concepts taught at earlier levels. New skills and concepts presented at this level include more advanced individual skills, changes in roles and relationships when three players (forward, midfielder, and defender) are added to make a third diamond, the expanded role of the goalkeeper, the use of more players in set plays, and various systems of play.

Individual Skills

Emphasize technical skills such as long passing, heading, and individual moves with the ball at this level. The players' size and strength now allow them to make long passes that were previously impossible. This ability adds a lot of diversity to their attacks. Always encourage them to make the longest passes possible without jeopardizing possession of the ball.

The players' ability to make longer passes also enables them to change fields quickly, which can devastate shifting defenders. Long passes allow them to cross the ball from the wing positions, thus developing the cross into a much more dangerous weapon.

Heading is another skill that should receive more emphasis at this level. By now players should have overcome most of their fears concerning heading. They should be aware that the ability to head the ball with precision allows them to maintain possession and increases scoring opportunities.

The repertoire of individual moves for creating space with the ball should expand at this level. Players need to continue to explore creative ways to change direction, speed, and levels with the ball as well as to develop their own bag of tricks.

Support

Young players often practice offensive techniques and tactics only when they are designated as offensive players. The opposite is true when they are designated as defensive players. All players, especially at this level, need to know that they have both offensive and defensive responsibilities. Naming positions, such as defender, is only a way of identifying players for the purposes of spacing and balance. There should be a team attitude that each player is a total player, capable of scoring when the opportunity presents itself or coming up with a big defensive play if that is what the situation demands.

Some coaches tell their defenders never to cross the midfield line for fear it will weaken the defense. Other coaches do not want their offensive players to recover to the defensive third of the field because it might affect a fast-break opportunity when they regain possession of the ball. And some coaches deny players the opportunity to make switching runs, which are movements by players to create space for maintaining possession of the ball and scoring opportunities. An example of a switching run might be a player making a diagonal run toward the side of the field from a more central position while a teammate simultaneously exchanges positions by moving from a position on the side of the field toward a more central position as in figure 6.3 (page 229).

You will diminish or eliminate creativity and mobility in the attack if you do not let your players make certain types of movements. Instead, give them opportunities for more mobility. This does not suggest that they should demonstrate reckless play in an "anything goes" style. The key to having players become more mobile is maintaining field balance. For example, if a defender makes an overlapping run to a forward position to create a numbers advantage, teammates must provide depth on defense by shifting their positions accordingly. You need to teach your players to play as a unit.

Retaining possession of the ball is still critical to the success of any team. The longer a team has the ball, the less chance the other team has of scoring. Ball possession is affected by the position of a player on the field and the risk factor associated with that position. Players who make lots of switching runs should be aware of the risk factors in each area of the field. Teach players in possession of the ball in the defensive third of the field to act swiftly to move the ball out of that area. Loss of possession in the defensive third is a critical situation. Warn players against excessive dribbling or dangerous passes, particularly in the middle of the defensive third of the field. It is generally more acceptable to make longer forward passes in this area, even if they are not precise than to risk loss of possession and a scoring opportunity for the opponent.

Encourage players in the middle third of the field, however, to risk loss of possession by making penetrating runs or passes. Occasional loss of possession in this area is not as dangerous, because there is plenty of space in which to recover.

In the offensive third of the field, let your players know that the more chances they take, the more they will score. Do not let them develop mental blocks about shooting. Encourage them to take on defenders with their individual moves and to be aggressive in shooting. Loss of the ball in this area of the field is not critical, because players have sufficient time to recover.

At this level, the addition of three players gives teams more flexibility in player movement. These three players (one forward, one central midfielder, and one defender) add a third diamond to the team formation (see figure 6.6).

Adding another forward player creates more opportunities to play the ball forward. It also increases the team's mobility, because more creative movements are possible in the offensive third of the field. The extra central midfield player provides another target for teammates in the defensive third of the field, relieving pressure during transitions from defense to offense. The extra midfielder also provides support for the attacking players, creates scoring opportunities through combination play with the forwards, and provides defensive balance when the other midfielders make forward runs. The addition of the third defender provides more support for the goalkeeper and other defenders and helps the midfielder relieve pressure.

233

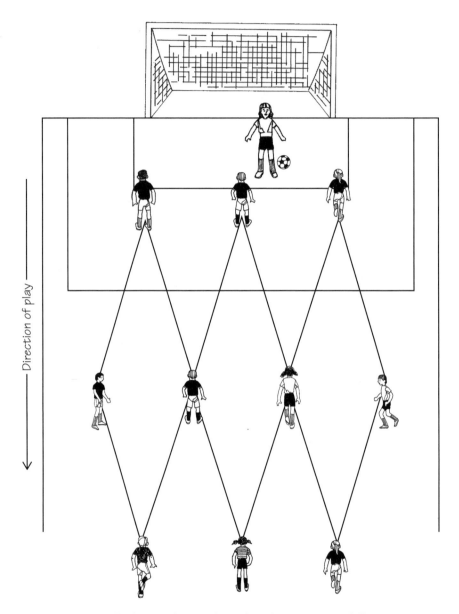

Figure 6.6 Triple-diamond team shape (11-player team model).

Goalkeepers must increase the level of their individual play at this level. Devote more practice time to goalkeeper preparation with drills that emphasize speed and reaction time. More specifically, these drills should involve variations on collecting, tipping, batting, diving, and clearing skills. The goalkeeper should also be involved

234

in lots of small-sided game play during practices, in which players use communication, movement, collection, and distribution skills to relieve pressure from defenders.

Play Systems

To add more structure to the 11v11 game, coaches implement certain play systems, or team formations. The system that a team uses reflects the philosophy of its coaching staff. The 3-4-3 system is one that players, using the progressions suggested earlier, learn easily. It provides opportunities for strong midfield and attacking play. However, you need to select a system flexible enough to accommodate the strengths of your players. Do not make the mistake of using a system that does not suit your players.

For example, if your team has two very talented attacking players but is not as strong defensively, you may decide to use a 4-4-2 system. This system allows for an added defender, strong midfield players, and two attackers. The 4-4-2 system is a bit more defense oriented. If you use this system, encourage your players to interchange positions and to make supporting runs, thereby generating more offensive opportunities.

If your team has several strong midfielders, a 4-3-3 system may be appropriate. This system has four defenders, three midfielders, and three attackers, which makes the team strong in defending and attacking but weaker in the midfield area. Strong play by the midfielders may compensate for this weakness.

Set Plays

The 11v11 game creates a situation in which there are 20 players, excluding goalkeepers, on the field. Therefore, when designing set plays to create scoring opportunities, you should focus primarily on spacing. All players should understand their responsibilities on each play to help the team maintain proper spacing and not become confused. The players at this level are bigger, stronger, and more highly skilled. Quick transition of the ball from one penalty area to the other is more likely. Do not make the mistake of moving too many players forward in attacking positions during free kicks. Such a maneuver makes the team vulnerable defensively, particularly if it occurs early in the game.

Remember that the progression from the beginning player, aged 5 or 6, to the player aged 11 or 12 is a long process. Always be fair to the players by giving them information that is appropriate for their current level of ability. Above everything, be patient throughout this learning process.

7

Using Drills in Practice

Practices should include a variety of drills, activities, small-sided games, and full-field games. All of them promote the development of both individual and group skills and concepts, which in turn leads to improved strategies and games. Use drills as an integral part of practices to develop a small part of the big picture. Drills enable the players to focus on one aspect of the game without the distraction of other elements.

Careful planning will allow you to use drills that are appropriate for your players and offer many opportunities for both movement and ball touches. When planning, choose drills to address specific areas of development. For example, if your team is having trouble scoring after moving the ball to the offensive third of the field, then practices should include drills that emphasize finishing skills.

Making Practice Drills Successful

Several key factors make drills work in practice. Plan to divide the group into smaller parts, change activities frequently, have sufficient equipment, vary formations, switch the order of activities, and make the drills gamelike.

Whenever possible, divide the players into small groups during drills. By using grids, you can identify the boundaries of general space for each group. In spacing grids, consider safety and your ability to observe adequately. Small groups of players within these grids will have opportunities for hundreds of touches on the ball during each practice. It is also a good idea to change combinations of players frequently so that every player gets a chance to play with every other player. Players in small groups accomplish more in shorter time periods, because they spend less time standing around. You also have the opportunity to present more activities during each practice session.

In general, spend no more than 15 minutes on a particular drill during each session. Changing drills frequently keeps players motivated, which increases their work rate. You must have sufficient equipment to implement lots of drills with smaller groups. Each team's equipment inventory should include a couple dozen small game markers of various colors, scrimmage vests, and a ball for each player. Small portable goals are helpful for drills (in addition to regular goals).

Switching the order of activities occasionally helps drill work go more smoothly. For example, players can work on a drill involving individual moves during the first part of the first three practice sessions. On the fourth practice session, you could start practice with a small-sided 4v4 game and follow with drills that develop individual moves. Breaking up practice routines keeps players motivated.

Changing formations regularly also gives a different look to drills. Alternately using triangles, squares, and circles for drill work adds variety. Varying the number of players, number of balls, and amount of space for drill work helps to promote a high work rate.

All of these strategies help keep kids attention when participating in drills during practice. Other strategies for keeping their attention include being prepared for practices, limiting dialogue, and giving visual demonstrations during coaching sessions. Little things such as having the players huddle during a teachable moment or facing them away from any distractions while they're being addressed also increase their attentiveness.

Probably the most important factor in the success of a drill is whether the players are having fun. Drills will be fun for players if you present them in a gamelike fashion. Many of the drills in this book have gamelike qualities. Using them in their proper progressions not only helps players develop skills and concepts but also makes them enjoyable.

The practices outlined on the following pages are broken down into age groups. The drills selected for each age group reflect the ability of the mythical "average" player of that age. You may feel, for example, that the drills designed for 7- to 8-year-olds are not appropriate for your particular team of 8-year-olds, because they are too challenging or don't quite stretch your players' abilities. Modify them as necessary. Also keep in mind that the practices presented do not include designated times for water breaks and stretching. Schedule such things into your practice where appropriate.

Practices for 5- to 6-Year-Old Players

Practices for 5- to 6-year-olds should last approximately 60 minutes. Each practice should include a variety of drills, activities, and small-sided games that promote the development of individual skills and concepts, group skills and concepts, strategies, and game sense. At this level, offensive skill and concept development is much more difficult than defensive development. Therefore, when organizing your practice plan, design drills that have no defensive pressure or passive defensive pressure. Always give the numbers advantage to the offense if there is a numbers differential, such as 3v1.

Develop a warm-up plan for your players, and follow it as they are arriving to practice. Include in the warm-up activities that involve various skills, including juggling, passing, dribbling, heading, and shooting. Players can do these activities without much instruction. They will tend to gravitate toward the shooting station, so encourage them to spend equal amounts of time at all the stations.

I recommend that at this level you use the 4v4 format for scrimmages. It is helpful to paint the goals different colors, such as red and green. During the game, have one team wear green jerseys and the other team red ones. The painted goals give the players a visual cue for determining direction. If other groups use the goals and painting is not allowed, simply tie a couple of green jerseys to the top of one goal and red jerseys to the other. If the teams switch sides at a specified time, untie the jerseys and place them on the opposite goals. If a players on the team are color blind, use jerseys with symbols.

You should not place players in this age group on regular teams. Regular teams suggest competition, and emphasizing competition too early minimizes the development of skills and concepts. Competition for 5- to 6-year-olds is like flu medication. If given in proper doses, it can be helpful. If given in too large a quantity, it can be harmful.

Each week, divide the players differently so they experience playing with all the other players. Tables 7.1 through 7.3 show three examples of typical practices for 5- to 6-year-old players.

TABLE 7.1

Practice for 5- to 6-Year-Olds

Type of activity	Content	Time
Large-group skill work	Personal Space Drill (3)	10 minutes
Large-group skill work	Fancy Footwork Drill (15)	15 minutes
Small-group skill work	Is Anybody Home? Game (19)	10 minutes
Small-group skill work	Thread-the-Needle Drill (37)	5 minutes
Large-group game	4v4 scrimmage	25 minutes
Large-group instruction	Closure	5 minutes

TABLE 7.2

Practice for 5- to 6-Year-Olds

Type of activity	Content	Time
Large-group skill work	General Space Drill (4)	10 minutes
Large-group skill work	Fancy Footwork Drill (15)	15 minutes
Small-group skill work	Follow-the-Leader Drill (16)	5 minutes
Small-group skill work	Good-Bye Drill (39)	5 minutes
Large-group game	4v4 scrimmage	25 minutes
Large-group instruction	Closure	5 minutes

TABLE 7.3

Practice for 5- to 6-Year-Olds

Type of activity	Content	Time
Large-group skill work	Volcano Drill (6)	5 minutes
Large-group skill work	Fancy Footwork Drill (15)	15 minutes
Large-group skill work	Intruders Game (23)	10 minutes
Small-group skill work	Hello Drill (42)	5 minutes
Large-group game	4v4 scrimmage	25 minutes
Large-group instruction	Closure	5 minutes

Practices for 7- to 8-Year-Old Players

Practices for 7- to 8-year-olds should last approximately 60 to 75 minutes. Continue to introduce players in this age group to skill techniques. Include drills that develop skill technique with no defensive pressure. These players are growing physically and mentally, so you can challenge them to incorporate more individualized team tactics into their play. The addition of a goalkeeper definitely changes the structure of both practices and games.

Scrimmages at this level should use the 5v5 format—four players in a diamond shape, plus a goalkeeper. Players at this level should be placed on regular teams. Encourage them to maintain the team shape during play. The emphasis during practice and game situations should be on long-term player development and not the short-term goal of winning. Tables 7.4 through 7.6 show three examples of practices for 7- to 8-year olds.

TABLE 7.4

Practice for 7- to 8-Year-Olds

Type of activity	Content	Time
Large-group skill work	Freeze Drill (18)	10 minutes
Small-group skill work	Monkey-in-the-Middle Drill (58)	10 minutes
Small-group skill work	Run-and-Shoot Drill, level 1 (80)	10 minutes
Large-group instruction	Explain role of goalkeeper in 5v5 play	10 minutes
Large-group game	5v5 scrimmage	20 minutes
Large-group instruction	Closure	5 minutes

TABLE 7.5

Practice for 7- to 8-Year-Olds

Type of activity	Content	Time
Large-group skill work	Freedom Drill (17)	10 minutes
Large-group skill work	Pendulum Drill (44)	10 minutes
Small-group skill work	Run-and-Shoot Drill, level 1 (80)	10 minutes
Large-group instruction	Explain role of flank players	10 minutes
Large-group game	5v5 scrimmage	20 minutes
Large-group instruction	Closure	5 minutes

TABLE 7.6

Practice for 7- to 8-Year-Olds

Type of activity	Content	Time
Large-group skill work	Circle Collection Drill (41)	10 minutes
Small-group activity	Circle Dribble Tag Game, level 1 (24)	10 minutes
Small-group activity	Pass-and-Shoot Drill (82)	15 minutes
Large-group instruction	Explain role of forwards in diamond formation	10 minutes
Large-group game	5v5 scrimmage	20 minutes
Large-group instruction	Closure	5 minutes

Practices for 9- to 10-Year-Old Players

Practices for 9- to 10-year-olds should last approximately 75 to 90 minutes. These players should have had experience playing 4v4 and 5v5.

Introduce the double-diamond 8v8 formation at this level. The game is more structured, and play should be intentional. Practice continues to emphasize the process of collecting, looking, and decision making. Introduce and reinforce the defensive concepts of cover and compactness as they apply to both the individual and the team. Also, emphasize principles of offensive play such as supporting teammates and using field width, which is integral to the development of more creative play at this level.

One of the most difficult concepts to teach players in this age group is how to deny space efficiently. Players at this level often believe that it is their responsibility to defend the entire field; thus, they often move to any space the ball goes to. If your entire team consists of this type of player, there will likely be a swarming effect during play. To alleviate this situation, teach the players about their particular field positions and how they relate to the other positions. At the same time, emphasize the importance of maintaining the double-diamond team shape.

Continue to develop the skills and concepts that players ought to have learned at earlier stages. Some players will have mastered these skills at a faster rate than others and be ready for the introduction of new skills and concepts. For those players who are not as ready, it may be helpful to offer alternatives for additional training such as the formulation of a home practice plan or extra practice sessions. Tables 7.7 through 7.9 show practice plans for 9- to 10-year-old players.

TABLE 7.7

Practice for 9- to 10-Year-Olds

Type of activity	Content	Time
Large-group skill work	Fancy Footwork Drill (15)	15 minutes
Small-group skill work	2v2 Keep-Away Drill (65)	10 minutes
Small-group skill work	Wall Pass Shooting Drill (93)	10 minutes
Large-group skill work	Explain double-diamond formation	20 minutes
Large-group game	8v8 scrimmage	25 minutes
Large-group instruction	Closure	5 minutes

TABLE 7.8

Practice for 9- to 10-Year-Olds

Type of activity	Content	Time
Large-group skill work	Four-Grid Scramble Game (33)	10 minutes
Small-group skill work	Partner Dribble Game (28)	10 minutes
Large-group skill work	1v1 for All Drill (94)	10 minutes
Large-group skill work	Explain role of two forwards in double-diamond formation	20 minutes
Large-group game	8v8 scrimmage	25 minutes
Large-group instruction	Closure	5 minutes

TABLE 7.9

Practice for 9- to 10-Year-Olds

Type of activity	Content	Time
Small-group skill work	Two-Cone Drill (46)	10 minutes
Small-group skill work	Check Out–Check In Drill (63)	10 minutes
Small-group skill work	3v1 Shooting Drill (86)	10 minutes
Large-group skill work	Explain role of central midfielder in double-diamond formation	20 minutes
Large-group game	8v8 scrimmage	25 minutes
Large-group instruction	Closure	5 minutes

Practices for 11- to 12-Year-Old Players

Practices for 11- to 12-year-old players should last approximately 90 minutes. Continue to develop and refine the players' individual skills and concepts at this level. The physical changes in players (in size, speed, and strength) present new strategic opportunities. Practices should include the exploration of creative solutions that adopt a more mobile approach to attacking the opponent's goal. This mobile approach calls for flexibility in the positioning of players, more complex concepts of width and support, and the introduction of new movement concepts.

Before you present these new opportunities, make certain that players have learned the skills and concepts at the 5- to 6-year-old, 7- to 8-year-old, and 9- to 10-year-old stages of development. If this progressive system has not been in place, go back as far as necessary in the development of skills and concepts to ensure that your players will have a positive experience while learning. Tables 7.10 through 7.12 show some practice plans for 11- to 12-year-olds. Remember, these practice plans are just a sampling of the variety of experiences available for players at this level.

The plans in tables 7.10 through 7.12 include time for 11v11 scrimmages. If you do not have enough players for 11v11, employ the 8v8 format. Another possible solution to this problem is practicing with another team. You may even want to vary your schedule so you have opportunities to practice with a number of other teams.

Whichever age group you work with, try to remember that your players spend considerably more time in practice situations than in games. Make the practices valuable and fun learning experiences that will keep the kids coming back to enjoy another day of soccer with their friends.

TABLE 7.10

Practice for 11- to 12-Year-Olds

Type of activity	Content	Time
Large-group skill work	Three-Team Passing Drill (55)	10 minutes
Small-group skill work	3v2 Line Game (67)	10 minutes
Large-group skill work	Never-Ending 3v2 Drill (95)	10 minutes
Large-group skill work	Explain role of three forwards in triple-diamond formation	20 minutes
Large-group game	11v11 scrimmage	25 minutes
Large-group instruction	Closure	5 minutes

TABLE 7.11

Practice for 11- to 12-Year-Olds

Type of activity	Content	Time
Large-group skill work	Three-Team Keep-Away Game (61)	10 minutes
Small-group skill work	Two-Teammate Passing Game (66)	20 minutes
Large-group skill work	Shooting Combination Drill (96)	20 minutes
Large-group skill work	Explain role of three defenders in triple-diamond formation	10 minutes
Large-group game	11v11 scrimmage	25 minutes
Large-group instruction	Closure	5 minutes

TABLE 7.12

Practice for 11- to 12-Year-Olds

Type of activity	Content	Time
Large-group skill work	Sprint Challenge Drill (26)	10 minutes
Large-group skill work	Six-Goal Game (34)	10 minutes
Small-group skill work	Shake-and-Take Drill, level 3 (25)	10 minutes
Large-group skill work	Explain role of four midfielders in triple-diamond formation	20 minutes
Large-group game	11v11 scrimmage	25 minutes
Large-group instruction	Closure	5 minutes

About the Author

For 37 years Jim Garland worked with children ages 5 to 11 as an elementary physical education teacher. For more than 20 years he coordinated summer soccer camps and clinics for Motion Concepts Summer Camps, where he coached teams from beginning to high school levels.

As an undergraduate at Towson University in Maryland, Garland earned Most Valuable Player and All Conference Awards for two consecutive years. In 1970 he was selected as Senior Athlete of the Year. He was inducted into the Towson University Athletic Hall of Fame in 1985.

Garland earned his master's degree from Morgan State University in Baltimore in 1978. He earned a National Soccer Coaches license from the National Soccer Coaches Association of America (NSCAA) in 1998 and a doctorate in youth and child studies from Nova Southeastern University in Fort Lauderdale, Florida, in 1999.

Garland has been an Olympic Development Soccer Program assessor for the state of Maryland and a featured clinician at the local, state, and national levels. He has been a member of the National Soccer Coaches Association of America; Maryland Alliance for Health, Physical Education and Recreation; American Alliance for Health, Physical Education and Recreation; United States Physical Education Association; and Association for Supervision and Curriculum Development.